# Divine
# Interventions
—— in an ——
# Ordinary Life

## A Book of Remembrance

## BETTY J. DENISTON

WESTBOW°
PRESS
A DIVISION OF THOMAS NELSON
& ZONDERVAN

Scriptures taken from the Holy Bible, New International Version®, NIV®. Copyright © 1973, 1978, 1984, 2011 by Biblica, Inc.™ Used by permission of Zondervan. All rights reserved worldwide. www.zondervan.com The "NIV" and "New International Version" are trademarks registered in the United States Patent and Trademark Office by Biblica, Inc.™ All rights reserved.

WestBow Press books may be ordered through booksellers or by contacting:

WestBow Press
A Division of Thomas Nelson & Zondervan
1663 Liberty Drive
Bloomington, IN 47403
www.westbowpress.com
1 (866) 928-1240

Because of the dynamic nature of the Internet, any web addresses or links contained in this book may have changed since publication and may no longer be valid. The views expressed in this work are solely those of the author and do not necessarily reflect the views of the publisher, and the publisher hereby disclaims any responsibility for them.

Any people depicted in stock imagery provided by Thinkstock are models, and such images are being used for illustrative purposes only. Certain stock imagery © Thinkstock.

ISBN: 978-1-4908-4286-8 (sc)

Library of Congress Control Number: 2014911771

Printed in the United States of America.

WestBow Press rev. date: 7/31/2014

# Contents

# Dedication

This book is dedicated to my Lord and Savior Jesus Christ, without whom there would be no story; to Eugene and Irene Johnson, my Mom and Dad who were such a vital part of these interventions, and to Dan Deniston, the love of my life.

# Preface

**INTERVENE:** *To occur or come between points of time or events (Webster dictionary)*
*To interrupt or to intercede (Roget's Thesaurus)*

Does Almighty God, Creator of this world and universe, actually intervene in the *everyday* circumstances of an ordinary life? Growing up, I'd not given that very much thought. I'd heard of occasional miraculous events in extremely desperate situations; or sometimes God did something extraordinary for celebrities who could influence thousands of people. But intervening in *my* life?

Hindsight has caused me to thankfully see just how much God Himself really did engineer many of my circumstances over the past fifty years. These extreme-to-me interventions were in different forms: circumstantial, through other people, through God's Word, His perfect timing, or the promptings of the Holy Spirit inside myself. There were **many** Divine interventions, and though separate instances, they were all connected through these years.

My hope and prayer in sharing my story, is for both believers and skeptics to know that this series of interventions goes far beyond coincidence or "just life." I believe God cares about our daily life here on earth as well as our eternal life. In my case, He was personally involved – for my good - when I didn't know the end from the beginning.

# Introduction

*"And we know that in all things God works for the good of those who love Him, who have been called according to His purpose."* (Romans 8:28)

My ordinary life started out in a family I'd compare to the good old sitcoms of the 1960's: you know, Father Knows Best, The Donna Reed Show, Leave it to Beaver. We were happy in our simple lifestyle - not dirt poor, but not well off. Dad worked, Mom was a stay-at-home wife and mother. My sister was born seven years after me. We loved Jesus, went to church regularly and lived a pretty uneventful life, until my junior year in high school.

The events unfolding in 1964 brought changes which affected each one of us in very significant ways. God's intervening touch at unexpected times and in situations beyond my control rocked my comfortable world. As I look back, I am so grateful for the way God worked everything for good, though I didn't usually see it at the time.

Come join me on my journey as I re-live my life - with new understanding.

# God Moves Me to Unexpected Places

## God's Timing Interrupts My Life

*"By faith Abraham, when called to go to a place
he would later receive as his inheritance, obeyed and
went, even though he did not know where he was going."*
(Hebrews 11:8)

Spring 1964
Queens, New York City
Happy Memories and a Great Plan

My senses are alive on this gorgeous spring day in my junior year at John Adams High School. The clean smell of fresh air with its gentle breeze relaxes me as I walk home. My happy-to-be-alive mood prompts me to pause for a moment to reflect on my blessings, something I rarely do.

(Perhaps God initiated that mind-set to prepare me for what He knew I would encounter upon opening the front door of my home.)

Flitting through my mind as I walk, are happy memories of this past school year. For one thing, I have two new girlfriends who moved next door last fall. During football season we faithfully and enthusiastically attended our school's games in all the boroughs of New York City. Traveling by ourselves to unfamiliar places via complex bus or subway lines was a new experience for me and kind of scary. My more adventurous friends gave me the boost of courage I needed, and I have to admit it was good for me as I tentatively spread my wings a little bit. Between the three of us, we managed to not get lost or mugged in some of, shall we say, the less desirable neighborhoods.

We'd temporarily lose our voices in the crisp autumn air as we cheered on the cutest football players. I began to feel like part of the crowd, a good feeling. Sometimes we'd walk home bellowing out somewhat tunefully our school song, while waving our blue and white pompoms over the highway overpasses. I'd never envisioned myself doing anything this bold or silly.

My friends have added zest to my somewhat boring life, and I now have more school spirit than all of the past years combined. My above-average grades come fairly easily to me, but *until now* I'd spent all of my time studying, driven by some sort of inner compulsion I don't fully understand.

Just a few more months of this semester, and I'm eagerly looking forward to becoming a senior in the fall, with all of its perks. I think I have created a great plan completely suited to my needs! Life for me is good and I'm feeling on top of the world. As I approach our home, the tantalizing aroma of one of Mom's good home-cooked meals quickens my steps.

## An Unwelcome Announcement

As I burst into the house with TGIF jubilation, I'm totally unprepared for the strange atmosphere which I sense immediately but can't quite define. I stop in my tracks when Mom and Dad quickly call my younger sister Judy into our living room and tell us both to sit down.

"Uh, oh," I think, "Something's up and it doesn't look good."

All eyes are on Mom, who looks uncomfortable, like she's dreading what she's about to say. As she clears her throat, my happy mood is waning by the seconds. Her shaky voice almost makes me miss her first words. I can already feel in my bones that this will be something big.

"Dad just found out that Sunshine is moving to Sayreville, New Jersey, probably within the next year. We don't know exactly when yet, but we're going to have to move to New Jersey. It's much too long a trip to commute, so we have no choice."

I hear this announcement as one long run-on sentence. Did Mom rehearse these words? Her tone is hard to decipher. I'm surprised at the blunt and matter-of-fact way she's speaking, which brings me into an instant state of confusion. My head spins dizzily while Dad just sits there quietly, as they both let the news sink in.

Mom looks relieved, now that the words are out. I'm wondering why she and Dad look calmer than I feel. They have always appeared to me to thrive on established structure and predictability. I know I certainly do. This is major upheaval!

Dad's been a machine operator for 18 years at Sunshine Biscuit Co., in Long Island City, a short drive from home. I know this has been a good, steady job and that he isn't trained for any other profession. This is bad news. It's apparent that he can't get a different

3

job in his line of work, close enough to home. Why doesn't *he* look more upset?

Moving to New Jersey is catastrophic in my mind, knowing it would disrupt my senior year and graduation. How can they be so calm – when *my* world is suddenly falling apart?

I've been working very hard at planning my future. This year, I'm carrying a double load of classes in a longer school day. Not really *my* choice, this was a result of a family meeting initiated by my guidance counselor last year. Her 'teacher-y' tone of voice irritated me to no end as she tried to convince me to pursue a teaching career. I've known since fourth grade that I want to be a secretary, and can't see why educators think of a secretarial career as being a second-rate profession for an honor student.

I may be shy, but I can stand my ground if I need to. So I emphatically told the counselor I was absolutely sure of my planned career. My parents backed me up, but at the teacher's impassioned request, I agreed to the additional required courses for college admission, in the unlikely event I'd decide to go. At least this plan got my teachers off my back. I feel like I won, you know? The extra courses are not a problem, and I've been loving the secretarial and business courses which I've already started.

**But all of that could change instantly if we have to move! No, this can't be happening!**

Judy's not saying much. I can't read her thoughts. Really, we're all just sitting in stunned silence for a few minutes. But I know how *I* feel! This totally unexpected news is giving me a headache and my stomach is churning.

# More Questions than Answers

"What are we going to do?" is all I can think to ask at this distressing moment. I don't hear any answers.

I want to understand everything that's suddenly before me, with countless "what ifs" frantically circulating in my mind. I've got to know *when* this is going to happen. In the space of a few short minutes, I'm trying to live out the whole next year in detail. The walls are starting to close in on me. I feel trapped and need to get some fresh air outside to clear my mind.

Among my jumbled thoughts comes the realization that I've just begun to feel like I "belong," with the help of my few friends. This thought hits me like a ton of bricks. I don't want to lose my best friend and neighborhood girlfriends, and have to start over! This move is not going to be a good thing, any way that I look at it.

Having lived in New York since birth, I know in my head that each one of us does not want to move to New Jersey. Yes, I know it's not just about me. But really – now? The timing couldn't be more terrible!

My heart is still pounding as I send up a popcorn prayer to God for a solution to this enormous problem. Will God do something for me? Does He even care where I graduate and where I live?

There must be something I can do. Maybe some drama would help - the contrast from my usually passively-obedient self should get their attention. I don't think Mom and Dad realize how traumatic this is for me. So I take a deep breath and come back inside to present my case.

"No, no, no! What about graduation?" I tearfully emote in true panic. Why don't they say something? Panic turns to anger as I now whine,

"I just <u>can't</u> miss my senior year at John Adams! You know how I've got all my classes worked out. I don't want to go to a new school for another year; you've got to <u>do</u> something!"

Mom smiles at me quietly. That irks me even more; she could at least look upset for me.

"We've talked to one of our neighbors who'd be willing to have you live with them in your senior year." Mom tells me who they are.

*"Oh, so Mom and Dad have been giving this more thought than I realized," I think. But I don't know these neighbors <u>that</u> well.*

Enveloped in fear and negative thoughts, I can't even imagine living with someone else for a year; and living alone is out of the question. I'm not quite seventeen, and definitely not ready to leave my Mom and Dad. So I'm ready to give my answer.

"I think that would be too strange and uncomfortable for me, and I don't want to leave you all, either." I feel tears again threatening to spill out.

"Betty, you know that God is always with us and will lead us one step at a time. Somehow He will work it all out."

*"Yeah, right."* Oops, I hope I didn't say that thought out loud

I know that Mom's words are an attempt to comfort me, but I think she's trying to convince herself, too. The understanding and compassion that I now see in her eyes help me cope, at least a little bit. I know she cares, but my mind is still whirling, looking desperately for alternatives.

# This House That I Love is My Home!

*My anguish over this move isn't just about school, graduation and friends, either. I love our home; it's comfortable and I feel very secure in it. I don't want to move! I know my family doesn't want to either. Isn't there some way we could stay here?*

I don't suppose a lot of 17-year-olds actually love their home, but I do. I vividly remember the enormous improvement in our living conditions when we moved here ten years ago. Our former cracker-box apartment was perched over a china shop and very close to the elevated portion of the subway. When we'd climb up and down the narrow, steep and dingy stairway leading to our tiny home, we could hear the china rattle below as the trains would come and go.

Sometimes we'd ease ourselves out of a bedroom window to have a 'picnic' supper on the hot tar roof to get a little relief from the oppressive summer heat. Only the rich had air conditioning in those days, and our little home was all Mom and Dad could afford then. I shared a small room with Judy, who was an infant at the time. Thankfully, we lived there only a year.

∼

Our present, much larger home, is two-story with a full semi-finished basement and enclosed front porch. It looks a lot like the opening theme scenes of the sitcoms "All in the Family" and "King of Queens," except for the fact that our house is not "attached" – there's a small driveway between each house on the long city block. But only compact cars can fit into it, so we have a shed instead of a garage out back and Dad parks at the curb in front.

It's still hot in the summer without air conditioning, but at least we get a breeze through our numerous windows. Dad uses every available inch of our small backyard to raise many varieties of gorgeous roses, other fragrant northern flowers, and delicious beefsteak tomatoes. I am very happy in this wonderful home, and thrilled to have my own, large room!

Our sweet, orange-striped tabby cat Tiger, whom we've raised from a six-week old kitten, has the run of the house during the day. Having retired from his youthful days of playing ping pong throughout the house, Tiger's a lap cat now. Every evening he stretches full length over my shoulder, purring in contented bliss. A significant part of the family, Tiger seems almost human at times. He brings me much joy, amusement and comfort.

When we say "night, night, Tiger" he calmly walks across the house to the steps leading to his basement bedroom. I wonder if our new home, wherever that is, will be as well suited for our cat.

I like my neighborhood and feel safe. Mom's best friend lives two doors down; mine lives two blocks away. Shopping is at our corner. This move is <u>not</u> going to be a good thing for any of us. I'm frightened at the thought of leaving. I just hope it all goes away.

Mom and Dad's weekend house-hunting trips to New Jersey (even before the exact date of Sunshine's move is known) have been fruitless so far. Nothing suitable for a family of four is available in their price range. Now a tentative date is finally announced, but finding a house for us is looking hopeless. What's going to happen and when? I am so frustrated with all this uncertainty!

# The Class Ring

Oh, great, another problem: I've just found out it's time to order my senior class ring for the next school year. Mom tells me we can't afford it, especially since it's likely I won't graduate from John Adams. I am *not* happy at this, another bombshell dropped on me! All my friends have excitedly ordered theirs. I feel deprived, but displaying teenaged angst doesn't change a thing. (It doesn't occur to me until more than a year later that I could have bought it with my allowance savings! For a smart person, I can be pretty dumb at times!)

I don't understand why all of this is happening to me, it's not fair! I pray but don't have any answers. Does God really care about this? Where is He in all of this?

# Senior Year at John Adams High

I was so excited when Dad brought home the best news ever a few weeks ago. Sunshine's move has been delayed for another year; so my senior year is unaffected! With a sigh of relief, I remembered to thank God for what I believe was a direct answer to my desperate prayers.

It's mid-September now, and I'm a very happy senior at John Adams. I'm particularly enjoying the secretarial courses I'm taking in a much shorter school day (thanks to my double load of classes last year).

Last weekend, we visited Grandma and Grandpa Johnson in Long Island. Grandma came out with a tiny box and I noticed her and Mom exchanging knowing glances.

"What's going on?" I asked, as they looked like they were about to burst. Grandma beckoned me over.

"Come here, Betty, I've got something for you."

In her hand was a John Adams class ring, but not just any ring. This one had belonged to her daughter, Eda, who graduated there *the year I was born*! Eda died a few years later, so I don't remember her. The ring's clipper ship black and gold design looks almost the same as the current one. I thanked Grandma and slipped it on my finger.

Of course I was glad to have this special ring, but now that I'm back at school and can see the difference, I feel embarrassed that it's not *exactly* the same as everyone else's. I know most people wouldn't look close enough to notice. I guess I just don't want to look different, or admit that we couldn't afford the 'real' one.

The more I think about it, the more my conscience pricks me into feeling a little ashamed about not acknowledging this 'miracle of the ring,' if you could call it that. To think that Grandma would have kept that ring all those years, not to mention remember where she'd put it, makes me wonder.

*Maybe God did prompt her to give it to me. I guess God really does care about little things like that and probably had a part in giving me the ring I wanted so much. And I'm probably the only senior in history whose class ring has their birth year on it!*

Having fewer classes makes school easy for me, and fun at times, as winter turns into spring. I begin to feel giddy – maybe it's spring fever? – when the really cute quarterback of our football team chooses to sit next to me in Music Appreciation, and I find myself helping him out as he struggles through the class. It feels really good to be sitting beside this popular guy, whom I've discovered has a hint of humility!

*I didn't really think I helped him that much, but later that year he wrote in my yearbook, "Thanks for coaching me through music." I smile when I think of that (even though he never asked me out or anything). I guess any male attention made me happy at that point.*

# Graduation!

## June 1965

Senior year has sped by, and I've enjoyed every minute. I'm so thankful and actually ecstatic to graduate from John Adams, with honors. Our graduation class of 850 students participates in an outdoor ceremony on the beautiful grounds of the high school. The blazing hot sun beating down on my heavy, dark blue gown doesn't faze me in the least. I'm so happy to have finished this chapter of my life! I feel almost overwhelmed with joy and freedom at the thought of no more classes or studying. I'm done with school!

I'm now enjoying a great celebration as many of us have come to the New York World's Fair with our families and friends. I'd been there when it opened in 1964, but you just can't see everything in one day.

The World's Fair is like a theme park, with countless exhibits and some ride-through adventures. It's futuristic, informative and entertaining. I particularly enjoyed the Monsanto 360-degree movie which made me feel like I was actually moving within the spectacular scenery. I was inspired to see Michelangelo's Pieta as a slow-moving conveyer took us past this holy sculpture.

Walt Disney's "audio-animatronic" Abraham Lincoln has more than 250,000 combinations of facial expressions, gestures and other actions – something none of us had ever seen before. It was so lifelike, they could have fooled me if President Lincoln hadn't been dead for a hundred years!

Superhighways with cloverleafs were concepts underway – another futuristic display to wow us.

What a wonderful day this has been; I had a blast! My life has really turned around. First graduation, and now this fun day at the World's Fair make this the happiest day of my life!

*I'm starting to really believe that it was God's perfect timing that enabled me to graduate from John Adams High. The move to New Jersey fades a little from my mind. Maybe we won't move after all, I'm dubiously hoping. I hope God intervenes somehow. I believe He can if He wants to.*

# God has Moved Me into the Working World of New York City

During the last part of my senior year, many of us were allowed to go into The City for job interviews during school hours. I thought I could get a job nearby, but quickly learned that the only decent paying jobs are in Manhattan. Most people call Manhattan "The City," though it's only one of New York City's five boroughs. Manhattan is the hub of everything financial.

My neighborhood in Richmond Hill, Queens, is more of a quiet suburb. I'd only taken a few subway trips into Manhattan, always with family or friends. I'm already nervous about facing job interviews, let alone going by myself into the Big City. I have detailed directions, but still feel a little scared. Okay, a lot scared.

In this generation, most high school students don't work before graduation. I've known for years that I want to work right after high school, but the beginning steps are pretty intimidating to think about now that the time is really here. Am I doing the right thing, so soon? I prayed briefly about this. I wonder if God has a specific plan for where I work, and when.

I think I just need some more courage. I've asked my school friend Mary, who lives around the corner, if she'd like to go with me. She's thrilled that I suggested it; I didn't realize how scared she is, too!

Our interviews are with different companies, so we part ways and plan to meet up for lunch when we're done. I'm pretty nervous as my three interviews loom ahead. You can't study for this, I have no experience and no earthly idea of what to expect. But I also feel excited at the prospect of beginning a career and earning an income. I take a deep breath with a quick prayer as I approach the first interview.

It's with an advertising agency on swanky Madison Avenue. Wow, this is big time stuff! Talk about glamour, glitz and hype! I'm dripping awe as I take in this very colorful and sophisticated, totally different atmosphere. I feel small and insignificant as I wait there in a cubicle after the interview. When the boss returns, he says I look like I've been praying. I think I was, but I didn't get the job!

The second interview with Kress (of Kresge's 5 & 10 stores) seems okay, but lacks most of the glamour of the first job. They just say they'll call me. Third time's a charm; the Port Authority hires me on the spot. I'm sure glad these interviews and tests are over and I can breathe again.

Mary and I have lunch at Horn and Hardart, the famous automat where food of all kinds is dispensed in a huge room of nothing but vending machines. This is a novelty in the 1960's, and is a fun experience. The food is better than you'd think. While enjoying our nice lunch and unique atmosphere, Mary tells me she's been hired at Con Edison Electric, not too far from my building. I'm not sure who's more excited, Mary or me, at this new beginning in our lives.

So now, just two weeks after graduation, I've started working as Clerk-Steno for the Port of New York Authority. The beginning salary and benefits are great, and I'm happily surprised (and relieved) to see that my job begins with a two-week orientation class of 50 young women. This is helping me transition from school into the business world. I still feel overwhelmed, but so do the other girls. It's nice to know we're all in the same boat.

*I think the Lord knew I would need this extra help; most businesses don't have that kind of extensive orientation. Our* instructors are wonderful to us and I'm happy to develop a few friendships out of this class. I see this as a blessing engineered by God.

We're all assigned to various departments during our one-year 'probation.' There's a lot to take in, but I find that the bosses, for the most part, are patient with all of us greenhorns.

After months of working in several different departments, I'm finally assigned to Electronics, which seems to be a good fit for me. I like the people and the variety of my work assignments a lot better than any of the previous offices (one of them I could hardly wait to get out of). After a few more weeks I'm happy to find out that this will be my permanent department when I complete my probationary period.

# Adjusting to Big City Life

The very first thrill of my job was payday, of course. Wow, this is real! I was overjoyed to have money to spend on myself; money was always tight in our family. Immediately upon leaving work that first Friday, I found myself shopping at an upscale Manhattan store, a brand new experience for me. I still remember buying that expensive black sheath long-sleeved dress with tan suede buttons and trim. I have to say that I look classy in it!

As I continue to establish a wardrobe, I see myself beginning to fit into this new and sophisticated environment of color-coordinated suits and dresses with matching shoes and accessories. I enjoy looking stylish and well dressed, and like my new look. *(This, of course, is the culture 'back in the day.')*

Manhattan is a very busy, fast-paced city with shoulder-to-shoulder crowds of people on the streets and an endless sea of taxicabs. If you hesitate, you'll get run over. The sounds of horns blaring and people yelling out of their vehicle windows permeate the air. I'm learning to move very quickly in my size 5 shoes. At least I don't have to leave my building if I don't want to.

I enjoy having lunch with my friends Vinnie (short for Vincenza), Dorothy and Rosalie, at some of the many Manhattan luncheonettes and restaurants. It's expensive, though, so we don't do it every day. We occasionally walk around the famous streets to window-shop or see the sights when the weather is nice.

We're not far from Greenwich Village, so my curiosity convinces my friends to explore the area with me during our lunch hour. Lots of art-related shops decorate the streets, as well as some artsy-looking people. I'm thrilled to see the Arc de Triomphe in Washington

Square. This is modeled after the one in Paris, which interests me because I took three years of French in school. So, voila!

Heading back to work, I notice that a weird and suspicious-looking man I saw on the way here appears to be following us. I quietly mention this to Vinnie and we pretend to not notice while walking a little faster. Thankfully, we lose him after a block or so. I suddenly realize how oblivious we have been to stranger danger while curiously taking in the sights. I find it surprising that not too many people have bothered us. Especially in Greenwich Village. We only went there once.

All this social interaction with my friends helps relieve any stress I feel on the job. My biggest challenge there is interacting with people of various personalities and hang-ups. I don't think I've been very ready for the real world. Some people take advantage of my naivety and tease me. I'm fair-skinned and blush frequently, which obviously embarrasses me but entertains some people. I hate it when people enjoy my discomfort, even if it is only 'good natured teasing' (so they say). This is all part of becoming an adult, I know, but that doesn't mean I like it!

In hindsight, I believe God knew I needed the experience of working in the New York business environment, for reasons I would understand years later.

I also think I was unaware, then, of how much God was with me every day. A young, petite 18-year-old in the Big City is fair game for unsavory people. How much had I been spared from, I wonder. I believe God watches over and protects me.

# Now *My* Job is Moving!

A worker from another department has called some of us down to the basement of the building to show us something important. My curiosity is piqued. As we enter the room, I can virtually feel this electrically charged atmosphere. A team of executives proudly shows us the plans for the soon-to-be-built World Trade Center. I'm amazed at this incredible to-scale model that features twin towers which will be over 1350 feet tall, along with several other buildings in this impressive complex.

Though I don't understand much about the technicalities of the architecture, I can tell that this is going to be something spectacular. I learn that this has been a passionate vision of the Port Authority for a long time. Now the brilliant minds and skills of its workers are in high gear to make this dream become reality. Everyone is so excited; they are almost ready to break ground. It should take a few years to build and then all of our offices will be moving there, occupying many of the floors of the towers.

This sounds exciting, but do I want to move? It seems like déjà vu, you know; Dad's job has already moved. I wonder when I will have to deal with *my* move. My family's move to New Jersey is still so up in the air. Why is everyone moving when I want to stand still?

Even though the WTC will still be in Manhattan not far from this location, I can foresee a lot of chaos in such a huge move. This is not very good news for me. Too many changes!

My mind is trying hard not to think about our eventual move to New Jersey. But it's dawned on me that I could successfully commute from New Jersey if I had to. The Port Authority is a bi-state agency between New York and New Jersey, so I'm sure the rapid transit system would be adequate, though certainly a longer, less convenient trip.

Would I have to take a bus to the PATH train, which I assume goes through a tunnel? The river between New York and New Jersey has to be crossed somewhere. I seriously doubt I'd drive the bridge – a virtual parking lot at rush hour. Not to mention that I haven't even gotten my driver's license yet!

There's a lot to think about, but like *Gone with the Wind's* Miss Scarlet, I'll worry about that tomorrow. Right now, life is pretty good for me.

# A Radical Move That's Made for Me

For almost a year now, Dad's been commuting to Sunshine on bus and subway for two very long hours each way (driving in New York traffic would take longer than that.) I can see the strain on his face and have noticed his slowed-down pace. There's still not a house for us on the horizon. I do feel sympathetic toward Dad, but I wonder, is God trying to tell them both something with these roadblocks? Mom and Dad are praying a lot, I know.

I'm surprised to learn later on that Mom's been secretly longing and praying to move to Florida ("The Sunshine State" – *how ironic*) since she heard of Sunshine's move. Her mother and stepfather moved to Hialeah, a suburb of Miami, several years before.

We'd vacationed there twice since then and Florida opened up a whole new world to us. The pure blue sky was a dazzling contrast to New York's often-dreary weather and smog. The palm trees, beautiful beaches, year-round warm weather, and a much slower pace from that "New York state of mind" lingered with us all, long after vacation ended. I really liked what I saw there. Though now forgotten, Florida probably still lies somewhere in my subconscious mind.

Mom told me afterwards that she'd never even mentioned this hope of hers to my father because she thought it impossible that Dad, who avoids taking any kind of risks, would even consider moving so far away without a job. He's 49 years old - not the best age to learn a new line of work. There are no factories in South Florida. What other kind of work would he be qualified for?

So Florida is the farthest thing from my mind when one morning Mom gently tells me that just before going to sleep the night before, Dad calmly said to her,

"You know, I think we should move to Florida."

"WHAT?" I almost scream.

At my shocked face, she quickly explains that John, our friend from church, suggested Dad apply for a job with the Post Office. John likes being a mail carrier and said the pay and benefits are very good. They're frequently hiring, and John told Dad he just has to pass a general aptitude test to qualify. It's certainly worth a try.

I don't know how much time passed between Dad considering applying at the Post Office in New York, and moving to <u>Florida</u> to take the test, but Dad told Mom,

"I think God is leading us to move to Hialeah; I think I can do this."

This is another bombshell in my radically changing life! I'm stunned by this news, and temporarily rendered speechless. Am I hearing right? Florida? I grab at something to steady myself. At least, my racing mind quickly tells me, we would have a place to live temporarily with Grandma and Grandpa.

Mom's calm demeanor, as she speaks, doesn't hide her excitement from me. She's very happy, but I'm not sure what to think.

This is a tremendous leap of faith for both my parents. I'm amazed, knowing that it has to be God who changed Dad's heart and thinking to courageously plan this big move. There's no other explanation; Mom could vouch for that! But in my convoluted way of thinking, I have to decide how I'm going to respond to this startling development. I have two options: Go with them or stay in New York.

On the one hand, I am drawn to Miami's warm weather in the winter months, an appealing contrast to the cold New York winters with heaters which dry up my nose, give me nosebleeds and dry itchy skin. All the homes in Miami are air conditioned, so I'd have no more intolerable New York summers without it. I do like Miami.

On the other hand, I've just gotten used to my new job and feel pretty comfortable with my friends at work, church and neighbors. My shyness prevents me from making new friends easily, and stresses me out. It's overwhelming for me to think about all the changes this move will bring. Having to go through job interviews again to find the right job still seems pretty scary to me.

*"Get real, Betty; there's no way you're going to stay here without your family!"* I tell myself. Not quite 19, I'm still a teenager and not anywhere near ready for life on my own. So I decide to approach this prospective move with hopeful anticipation, though still feeling somewhat fearful with the unknown looming ahead.

Judy is eleven. She doesn't have a choice either, but she adjusts to change easier than I do. She lived with our grandparents in Hialeah one winter a few years prior, when the doctor ordered a warm climate to cure her severe respiratory problems. That experience helped her rapidly adapt to new circumstances, and she also became closer to our grandparents, especially Grandpa Martinez. Judy seems okay with this move.

All of us pray briefly together before our supper meal, and though still apprehensive, Mom and Dad believe God is engineering this move and prepare to pull up roots and go.

I'm surprised at myself when suddenly the idea of living in Miami begins to at least *seem* to be a good thing for me. In fact, a few ongoing things I've encountered on and off the job in Manhattan have bothered me. I can't really put my finger on it, but I unexpectedly feel a sigh of relief at the thought of leaving New York. Could this be God intervening in my mind? The fact is, we <u>are</u> moving, so I'll rev up my normally optimistic nature and look on the bright side. I'm sure there are lots of secretarial positions in south Florida.

Still a teenager, I am not yet a strong person of faith. Though my faith has been slowly developing through these events, I am still waiting to see how all of this is going to play out for me. The unknown is what's bothering me the most; I usually have my life pretty much planned out.

I think I'm starting to believe that this move is really God's intervention, but I still wonder why. The Lord, however, is working out detailed plans behind the scenes. As the years continue, I begin to see how significant this move is for me in many different ways, when life for me changes more times than I could have anticipated.

# Blackout!

## God's Protection Intervenes in My Behalf

*"The Lord will keep you from all harm - He will watch over your life; the Lord will watch over your coming and going both now and forevermore."* (Psalms 121:7-8)

November 9, 1965
New York City
The Subway

*As I ponder this upcoming move from New York and my experiences in Manhattan, my mind goes back to a significant day when God left me no room for doubt that He was watching over me. But you have to be familiar with the area to know what I'm talking about.*

Newcomers to New York City soon find out that taking the subway is the only sensible way to get to work in Manhattan. Fortunately for me, my commute into the city is simpler than most. I walk two short blocks to the elevated portion of the subway. This is the beginning of the line, so I'm happy to have my choice of seats. It was a nice surprise to find out that the station where I get off takes me right into the Port Authority building - a big bonus in New York winters, rainy days and hot summers.

If you've never traveled on New York subways during rush hour, take it from me, this is an experience like no other. As a first-time rider, I quickly realized that it's critical to pre-plan the exact amount of time it takes from where I'm seated, to reach the doors when they open at my stop. The many bodies hurriedly shoving both in and out of the doors often force me to elbow my way through, sometimes in a panic that I'll not make it out in time. I'm definitely not an aggressive person, but the doors don't stay open very long, and I sure don't want to have to get off at the next station and wait for a train going back!

I'm glad the Port Authority's working hours are 15 minutes before the usual 9-5, giving me a little head start on the great homeward-bound rush and a better chance to find a seat. Sitting down is essential to me, since I'm only 5'2", and the handgrips are just about out of my reach. I try to avoid holding onto the ceiling-to-floor pole in the middle of the car; with so many hands there, that's more up-close and personal than I wish to be! The ride is not smooth in any sense of the word, and sudden stops can give me quite a jolt, especially if I have nothing to hold onto when I am standing. But there's little chance of falling down when surrounded by wall-to-wall people.

To pass the time, I read books during this 45-minute trip. This seems to discourage undesirable people from bothering me. The scariest part for me is when the subway car is virtually empty at the beginning of the line when I get on, or near the end of the line when I'm almost home. Sometimes I'm the only other person in the subway car. I never know who is going to share that car with me, and don't always feel safe. So far, so good, though.

It's around 5:15 p.m. The subway is now at one of its Brooklyn stops en route to my borough of Queens. I think it strange that the train is still sitting in the station way beyond the usual time. It's not unusual for the train to stop for five minutes or so, but that's always been *between* stations, when another line is changing tracks. Those delays usually happen when we're under the Brooklyn Bridge (a scary thought). Staying stopped at the station is <u>not</u> normal, and the doors are still open.

# I'm Not Seeing Clearly

The lights flicker, and I guess the backup auxiliary lights have come on in the train and in the station. I notice people curiously looking around. Soon I hear an announcement that there are some technical problems, but we should resume shortly. I try to settle down and read my book, but something tells me this is not a problem with a quick fix. Constantly checking my watch now, I'm starting to feel nervous. Waiting for any kind of information is now increasing my stress level incrementally with each passing minute.

Finally an announcement states that there's been a citywide blackout and we'll have to find some other means of transportation. That's all he says.

"What other means?" I ask myself in confusion. There are no other instructions or help for those of us who don't know where to go. A little panic sets in. Well, maybe a lot of panic. Oh no, what am I going to do?

I am not at all familiar with Brooklyn, and have no earthly idea of where I am and how to get home from here. All the people from the train are total strangers. New Yorkers in the 1960's are not friendly. No one offers to help me, a very young, just-turned-18 tiny person – and scared to death! I feel so completely alone amidst this crowd of people. Desperately, I turn to the person nearest me.

"What happens now? What should I do?" I hope she can help me.

She shrugs her shoulders. "I don't have a clue. But we have to get outside, now." She disappears into the crowd.

I see a pay phone close by, but the line is very long (cell phones haven't been invented yet). It would be reassuring to call my parents; maybe they could tell me what to do. But then I hear someone yell that the phones are dead. What now? This all seems like a blur of unreality to me, and I have no time to process the worry I feel. I just know I have to get out of there. How to get home is beyond me. I feel so lost! Finally I remember to breathe one of those quick panicky "God help me" prayers.

# Help is On the Way!

I do the only thing I can think of, just follow the herd of people pushing me up the subway stairs to the outside world. Then a miracle appears (at least to me, it is). There's a city bus stopped right in front of me, with the door open. I can hardly believe it when the driver tells me he's going to Queens! Better yet, his bus route includes my neighborhood of Richmond Hill! To add to this miracle, when I give my street address to this kind and smiling bus driver, he says he knows *exactly* where I live. He tells me when we've reached my stop and points me in the right direction. I'm dropped off about a mile from home, so thankfully, I know where I am now.

There are hundreds of bus lines in New York City. It's not mere coincidence that this bus which suddenly appeared before me was going so close to my destination. I consider this Divine intervention.

It's a good thing I know the neighborhood pretty well, because it's a cloudy, progressively darkening, damp November night, nearing 7:00 p.m. The streetlights are out; only a few occasional car headlights break the darkness. Although the crime rate explosion hasn't yet hit our suburb, it's still not a great neighborhood for a young woman to walk alone in at night.

I'm feeling pretty scared, and the shadows looming along the way make me think of lurking criminals. I hope no one is following me – I'm afraid to look behind me at the footsteps I hear. I've forgotten that God is with me as I nervously rush home as fast as my high-heeled shoes can carry me.

Relieved but exhausted, I arrive home safely. I think I must be in a mild state of shock. Mom and Dad have been frantic with worry;

I'm about an hour and a half late. All of us thank God that I made it back in one piece.

Mom tells me later that Judy was very worried about me. "So my little sister loves me after all," I think. Yeah, I know she does, but we've not been very close, having completely different personalities and being seven years apart. And she's only eleven. None of us in our family are overly affectionate, though we definitely love each other. It gives me a warm, fuzzy feeling to *hear* that Judy really does care, even if it is second-hand.

# It Could Have Been Worse

We learn from the radio that most of the northeastern coast has lost power. An overloaded transmission line coming out of the Ontario/New York border had a ripple effect, shutting down power to over 30 million homes. Most of the outages (including ours) lasted for 13 hours.

Hundreds of people working later hours in the skyscrapers of Manhattan were forced to walk down countless flights of stairs in the dark. Many people in various parts of the city remained stranded there overnight, including some of our family friends.

I feel my state of shock beginning to thaw as I transition into immense relief. I'm very glad I was spared from being stranded in the City overnight, but my emotions are still all over the place, reliving the trauma, and thinking about what could have been. I find out more the next day when my friend Mary calls me.

"Hi, Betty; did you get home okay yesterday?"

I tell her about my miracle bus driver. By now I'm really excited about how this happened. I almost forget to ask her how she fared.

"Oh, that's good." The hesitation in her voice makes me realize her experience wasn't so good. "I had a big scare. We were between stations and I had to walk along the narrow, dark and smelly catwalk to get to the next station. When I got outside, a guy attempting to steal my purse knocked me to the ground."

"Oh no, are you hurt badly?" I feel so bad for her.

"No, just some bumps and bruises. I'm still kind of shook up. But I made sure he didn't get my purse!"

Wow, I can just imagine my gentle friend battling a man over her purse. I can tell that she's still pretty traumatized over this incident. It makes me doubly grateful that I came through this event unscathed.

Though the power remains out overnight, within two days everything quickly returns to normal. It's amazing how life goes on as usual, in record time. New York is a resilient city!

I am so thankful for God's protection and provision throughout this entire experience.

I didn't realize until many years later how much God protected me that entire year as I rode the subway alone. How innocent and vulnerable I was then. I certainly was not streetwise, and needed God's protection daily. I still do.

So my faith is growing, though I tend to worry about life in general. God will continue to teach me to trust Him in all things through my approaching unknown but changing circumstances of 1966.

# The Big Move

## God Engineers the Circumstances of My Family

*"Trust in the Lord with all your heart and lean not on your own understanding; in all your ways acknowledge Him, and He will make your paths straight."* (Proverbs 3:5-6)

July – September 1966
New York to Miami
The Move and God's Interventions

July 5, 1966. Our move from New York to Miami is not without drama. I'm astonished when the people who bought our house start moving in the day before scheduled, while we're still living here. They stubbornly refuse to wait, even though our moving company comes tomorrow. The mix-up is their fault; what gall! It is total chaos around here. Their boxes and ours are intermingled everywhere. None of us knows if we're coming or going, literally!

I'm anxiously watching Mom frantically pace the floor throughout the house. She's praying loudly and crying. I think she's having a nervous breakdown; Mom's nearly hysterical. Mom's best friend shakes her, tells her to get a grip and eventually calms her down. Everyone's stress level is off the charts.

With great effort on everyone's part, things become somewhat organized, though I feel like I'm more in the way than helpful. Mom and Dad stay with our neighbor, and Judy and I spend the night with our grandparents (Dad's side) in Long Island, happily away from all the turmoil.

As my private teenaged thoughts mull about, I have a hard time connecting Mom's faith with her extreme reaction of anxiety and trouble coping. She was a basket case, in my opinion. I want my life to be peaceful and calm and don't know how to react when people around me are upset. Mom's name, Irene, means peace, and she strives for it, but I can't see that she always has it. Why is that?

July 6. As soon as the movers leave, Dad picks Judy and me up and we all take off in our un-air-conditioned car, in 102-degree weather, for this 3-day, 1300-mile trip to Hialeah. We make frequent water stops to quench our constant thirst and to hydrate. We splash some of the water on our faces and necks to cool off. The heat is oppressive and I almost feel sick; I don't sweat enough to cool down sufficiently. Judy is recovering from some minor surgery, so these miserable conditions increase her discomfort. Not ideal conditions for any of us. At least we're getting along reasonably well.

I still remember the interesting series of Burma Shave signs along I-95, and the South of the Border tourist pit stop with its interesting, funny advertisements miles before you get there. At least that occasionally breaks up the boredom as we plod along.

Tiger, on the other hand, has it made. He is on a flight to Miami (air cargo) and the pilot is watching over him in the air-conditioned airline office until we can pick him up!

Fortunately for all of us, the miserable road trip is safe, and on July 8, Mom's birthday, we arrive at our destination tired, hot, but glad we're finally here! It's a birthday gift of the best kind for Mom, her dream come true. I haven't decided yet if it's a gift for me.

The next day we reunite with Tiger, who shows no signs of trauma, and all of us live with my grandparents until Mom and Dad can buy a house.

As I reflect back many years later on Mom's New York moving day panic, I've now learned that it's okay to be human when you're a Christian. We're not perfect – not even our faith is – and that's why we need to rely on the Lord to give us grace as we move through changing circumstances. I personally witnessed Mom's deepening faith years after this move. This faith would be critical for her survival later on.

I understand now that faith isn't a one-time thing. It has to be lived one day at a time, as God works in my heart. I have to continually relearn this hard lesson as I deal with my perfectionistic thinking.

# A Stormy Beginning

Our first few months in Hialeah are in hurricane season, and I suddenly become an amateur meteorologist as Hurricane Inez heads across the area in late September. I watch and analyze the weather reports, plotting the storm with the limited information available (years before The Weather Channel and instant Doppler radar). It doesn't look too bad, but you never know.

Still living with Grandma and Grandpa, I anxiously watch Dad and Grandpa methodically pull down all of the hurricane awnings. Better safe than sorry; all the windows in the house are now covered. I'm comforted by this protection, but still a little worried about this new, impending event.

To be honest, I also find hurricane watching a little exciting. Dad has a sense for when the eye of the storm is passing above us, so I eagerly follow him outside when the time is right. It's eerily quiet and the sky looks very weird, kind of unearthly. I quickly follow my family inside; you never know how fast the storm will hit.

It looks and feels like a tomb in the house, and suddenly I can hear the 70+ mph wind howling with its relentless pounding rain. Some flooded water starts to seep into the front porch and onto its hard terrazzo floor. I'm working up a sweat mopping buckets of water for a while, passing each bucket along like an assembly line. (The power is out and so is the air conditioning; my hurricane excitement has suddenly vanished.) Fortunately, the porch is slightly lower than the rest of the house, so the seeping water has stopped there.

The storm leaves quicker than I thought it would. When I go outside, I don't really expect to face a war zone scene, but I'm surprised to see that the only significant damage beyond the usual flying debris is a small tree smashed to the ground. I'm glad it's now over and we can see daylight again. I'm very glad the power is already back on, along with the air conditioning.

We thank the Lord that He kept all of us safe. Even though it was only a Category I hurricane, it's something new to us, and we're relieved. Actually, the anticipation was worse than the event. I think there's a lesson there, somewhere.

# Dad's Now a Postal Worker!

The day after we arrived in Hialeah, Dad applied for a position at the Post Office. He was extremely nervous because he's never been good at taking tests. Having a job is crucial for Dad, who has always been the sole provider for our family. This move has truly been made on the wings of a prayer.

Waiting for Dad's results was especially hard because he came home that day afraid he might have failed the test. It was not easy, not what he expected.

"The mail's here" I announce as I anxiously run to the mailbox. Enough time has passed and I have a feeling Dad's test results are here.

I tear through the mail and there it is. I'm so excited, I hold the envelope up to the sunlight and can see his passing grade right through it. Waving the envelope high into the air, I run inside to find Dad.

"Dad, you passed! Hope you don't mind that I saw the grade through the envelope," I mischievously smile. He looks so relieved and happy. This is a definite answer to prayer and we all give heartfelt thanks to the Lord.

We pray together for Dad as he starts his new job as a letter carrier in September, just two short months after our move. He struggles at first, but eventually does so well, that some co-workers ask him to slow down so they won't look bad in the eyes of the supervisors.

Dad starts with a walking route, where he can "park and ride" his bike along the way. This physical nature of his job keeps him healthy.

Later on he will drive a mail scooter or mail truck, but will still get exercise, sometimes running from dogs "gone postal."

I'm happy to see a new side of Dad, as he becomes more outgoing in this line of work. Many of the people on his route connect with him. I'm glad to see him happier and more relaxed than he was in New York. I get a kick out of watching him at Christmas time when he excitedly flips open the lid of his lunchbox to see all the cards with money pouring out. We have fun counting it all; one Christmas he collected $500! He also receives homemade gifts from some of the people on his route.

This Post Office job blossoms into a fifteen-year career with salary and benefits far superior to his previous job. His wonderful health insurance and other benefits will be a lifesaver later on. I'm starting to see that God had a plan to intervene in Dad's mind not just to move from New York, but also to put him into this new line of work.

# Home, Sweet Home

In October, Mom and Dad buy a house two blocks from Grandma and Grandpa. This is amazing: what took almost two *years* of house hunting in New Jersey with no results, falls into their laps in just over two *months* in Hialeah, Florida. Was the Lord in this? Mom and Dad give God the credit.

I like this 3-bedroom house, with its pastel colors and tropical look. Not having a basement takes some getting used to, but I have a half bath in my bedroom. That's a big plus for me! Our home is not as big as the New York one, but this large corner-lot property with two gorgeous Royal Poinciana trees makes up for it. Sometimes in May when the trees are in full bright-red bloom, people stop and take pictures.

We have banana trees in the backyard. Dad also grows delicious, blazing-red beefsteak tomatoes; the one he just picked weighs exactly one pound! We're in a nice neighborhood and feel safe. We go to the beach occasionally, which is only about a half-hour away.

Our entire property is fenced in, and Tiger learns to be an outdoor cat during the day. He often takes catnaps under the birdbath! Since he'd spent most of his life indoors, guess he doesn't know that cats chase birds; so Tiger and the birds peacefully coexist. It's funny to watch them from the window. Tiger is a very unique and much-loved cat, and brings me and my family 21 years of fun and companionship. I think of Tiger as <u>my</u> cat because we have such a strong connection.

$\sim$

Well, my first impression is that I like my new home and environment, but my life seems to be more about "us" than "me" so far in this move. I have to agree with my parents though, that it's really the Lord who provided this home for us so quickly and so close to my grandparents. This will prove to be even more of a God-send when Grandma and then Grandpa will later need considerable help from Mom and Dad, as they develop major health issues.

# Divine Intervention for Judy

God also intervenes for my sister who moves into Junior High in the fall of 1966. God's guidance might be a better way to put it, but I believe God is involved in Judy's new school life in Florida. She maintains good grades, though the change from New York schools is quite significant. She becomes very proficient in Spanish, an almost mandatory language to know in Miami, and she is still current in the language 47 years later.

Judy has a special love for Latino people, stemming from her strong connection with Grandpa Martinez. Today she ministers to multicultural people through her church. Judy has her own story of many miraculous interventions by the Lord, also.

I already know that God really does answer prayer, but as a teenager, now 19, I am still waiting to see His plan for me. I have to believe He will intervene for me in finding a job, and in helping me find my place in this new world.

Through Dad's experience, I slowly begin to learn that I don't have to always be in control, or have everything figured out. Sometimes I just have to wait for God's guidance and His timing. With my personality, this is a great challenge!

# Working into God's Plan for Me

## God Opens and Shuts Doors, and
## Rescues Me from Disaster

*"The Lord will fulfill His purpose for me; your love, O Lord, endures forever."* (Psalm 138:8a)

1966-1967
Miami, Florida

From the moment I arrive in Miami, I feel sure that I'll have no trouble being hired for a secretarial position. Hopefully, it could be at the Miami Port Authority, like a transfer or something. Surely my past job would give me an edge. I quickly learn not to make assumptions. The Port Authority is a Lee County government position and there's a waiting list just to take their test. I don't want to wait that long; guess I'll try something else.

I've found some leads in the newspaper want ads, but my heart sinks when I see the number of women applying at each office. After passing the typing and steno tests, if you're lucky, you'll get an interview. Why do the many companies in downtown Miami not take me seriously? I know I'm a proficient stenographer and typist; I just can't understand why no one wants me. I was in the top 20% of my graduating class, for goodness sake! These "don't call me,

45

I'll call you" responses are wearing thin on my usually optimistic nature. I am indignantly surprised that most businesses prefer a college graduate. Should I have gone to college, after all? Or am I too young? I wonder if God is going to find the right job for me. I've been praying.

~

It's Friday. I'm finally at what looks to be a serious job prospect, having gotten to the interview stage. As I approach the office of an executive in a land management organization, I feel hopeful. Yet there's something about this very good-looking, polished man that makes me nervous, as he shuts the door behind me.

"I'm very *impressed* by your typing and stenographic abilities," he begins, in a smooth tone that I think borders on flirtatious (and maybe being impressed with himself).

Then he stops talking and just stares at me, for what seems like eternity. I realize with some relief that his stare is not a leer (though I wonder about his body language in the way he'd shut the door). I don't know what to think of this unusual interview so far. I'm suddenly aware of my face turning all shades of red. I'm sure he's observing this and I wonder if he can hear my heart pounding. What do I say or do? I just sit and wait, clueless. I mean, he's the one supposed to do the talking, right?

After this longer-than-pregnant pause he says, "I just wanted to see how you'd react under pressure."

Though I instantly feel I've probably blown it, he tells me I have the job because of my unusually good steno and typing results. I verbally accept, with paperwork to follow on Monday. I should feel relieved, but I have a vague uneasiness invading my mind. The pay and benefits are pretty good, though, and I've had no other offers, so why not.

In the meantime, Dad, who drove me there, has been sitting on a bench near the elevator. I'm surprised to find out that my usually reserved, 'don't make waves' father has been diligently watching and listening to the people heading out on their lunch break. After I tell him about the interview and my reaction he says:

"From where I was sitting, I heard a lot of negative comments and scuttlebutt from some employees as they were waiting for the elevator. More than just the usual work complaints, they seem to really hate their jobs. I'm wondering if you should accept this job. I've got bad vibes, even before you told me about your interview." He really looks concerned for me.

That's all I needed to hear. I call the office as soon as I get home and quit before I've started! I'm thankful I hadn't signed any papers yet. Was this Divine intervention?

I found out later that this position could have turned unethical or even dangerous for me. Some shady practices of the company were revealed in the newspaper a year or so later and they eventually went out of business. God used my own uneasiness and Dad's input to promptly turn the job down.

# Back to Square One

What am I going to do now? It's late September. I thought I'd be employed before Dad was; he's already started his job. I've enjoyed playing around in the Florida sun, but it's high time I started working for a living. My mind starts revving up into high gear, trying to figure out my next step.

Oh, wait; I remember that I took and passed the U.S. Civil Service test in high school. I find the forgotten paper surprisingly quickly, considering our New York moving chaos, and call the number on my certificate.

After receiving my official paperwork a week later, I look in the blue pages of the phone book for federal agencies. I can hardly believe this; the first one I contact has a vacancy and I'm called in for an interview right away. This interview is nothing like the last one, and I feel assured that this is a safe place to work.

# Finally Employed!

On October 12, 1966, Columbus Day (not yet a Federal holiday), I begin to work in downtown Miami for the U.S. Railroad Retirement Board. It's only a clerk-typist position - a slight disappointment. My goal is to be a secretary, but I guess it's a start. Working for the government has great benefits, and it's a pretty good beginning salary for an entry-level typist. I'm happy to have a job, but I hope there's potential for advancement.

The first assignment I'm given on my first day on the job is to walk three or four blocks from the federal building to another office for the required new employee fingerprinting. I quickly find out that my stylish high-heeled pumps with pointed toes are not good walking shoes. My heels are becoming painful, and on the way back to the office I can see blood beginning to appear around the back of my shoes. By the time I'm back in the office, I feel like I've run a marathon. I find it amusing (after the pain subsides) that my first item of business here is to find a first aid kit. Maybe it's an omen that this job will be my Achilles heel!

Though initially grateful to be employed, I'm not happy working in this small office. My boss and two co-workers have very quirky personalities and work habits that keep me on edge more often than not. Some of the clientele are, putting it nicely, quite different from people I'm used to being around. Sometimes I don't know how to respond to them on the phone or in person. I am becoming more uncomfortable each day, and wonder why God put me in this unpleasant job.

My typewriter is an outdated manual one – you know, those individual keys that stick up into the air and can cause your fingers to slip between them. This, plus the other antiquated office equipment, makes my workplace appear ancient, even for 1966. The equipment in my high school was better than this! The work I do is dull, monotonous and boring, if you get my drift.

We don't interact with other offices of this high-rise building. This part of downtown Miami almost reminds me of New York. I'm disappointed at the unfriendliness of the people whose paths I occasionally cross, and I'm too shy to pursue a friend. I haven't found much that's good in this job.

# The Bus

My unhappiness extends to another drawback: the long bus ride to work. I don't have a driver's license or car yet, because we didn't have Driver's Ed in school, and I'm still learning to drive. I took a few lessons in New York, but parallel parking is my biggest challenge; I still need more practice. Public transportation in Miami isn't as convenient as I had it in New York.

I hate this hour-long bus trip from Hialeah to downtown Miami every day. I'm kind of embarrassed when one woman who rides daily tells me to smile and asks why I never do. I didn't realize how much that showed. I read books to keep from going crazy, though the many bus stops are distracting. I tend to cautiously watch who's getting on, especially if the seat beside me is empty.

After awhile, I get to know some of the friendlier female regular riders. This became really helpful when one of them rescued me from an awkward situation I found myself in. A man sitting beside me sneakily started to have roving hands while I was reading my book. Though it slowly dawned on me what he was doing, I hesitated a bit to take action. I'd never encountered a situation like this before and didn't quite know how to handle this. My bus friend saw what was going on and stepped in to help me out. Still very young and innocent at 19, I'm learning about the real world each day. It's not always pretty.

My growing aggravation at the 10-15 minute wait I endure while the bus drivers switch in the middle of my going-home route is wearing on me. So I finally decide to do something about it. I mull around the thought of writing a letter to the County. Wait, this should be a group effort. Creating a petition to circulate among the regulars on our route seems the logical course of action. To my own astonishment, 20 of them sign it!

Not long after I mailed it to the county's transportation office, I happily notice that the bus driver is not stopping to switch drivers at the usual place on our route! I'm amazed that my effort had such a quick and lasting result! I guess sometimes one person can make a difference. The other people appreciated my efforts. It sure is nice to have a little shorter bus ride going home now.

# God Moves Me, Again

It's almost a year since I started working at this job that hasn't gotten better. I am miserable, and the stress is now affecting my physical and mental health. This is not at all what I'd envisioned my secretarial career to be. There's no chance of advancement in this tiny office.

Yes, I know I don't have a lot of work experience, but I really don't think I'm being too picky. You'd have to be there, you know? Saying I hate mostly everything about this job is an understatement. Why did God bring me here? I don't know how much longer I can stand it. I pray, but don't have any answers yet.

~

Eleven months into this miserable job, I share my angst with a family friend at church. He's an air traffic controller for the Federal Aviation Administration at the Miami Air Route Traffic Control Center. He tells me there are quite a few secretaries in the large facility, and suggests I contact the office. I'm overjoyed that they have an immediate opening for a clerk-steno! Because it's a federal position, I can transfer with little hassle. Better yet, it's a promotion and closer to home. By then I have my license and a car, so I can drive to work in about 15 minutes.

I'm put into a clerical pool of three stenos and a supervisor. I'm so happy that the typewriters are electric and the office is modern. The office windows make the atmosphere bright and cheery. This is so much better. The people are nice and I have a friend to go on breaks and lunch with. I am grateful!

It's occurred to me that perhaps the first federal agency I began working for merely got my foot in the door, as a step in God's plan to get me where He really wanted me to work.

I also saw first-hand how God used a friend from church to move me into a job much better than I expected. (Does this sound familiar? Remember Dad? The similarity is not lost on me.) I thank the Lord profusely.

## Yet Another Move!

This job is a lot easier to adjust to, and I'm happy here. After a few years, I am thrilled when our positions are reclassified from Clerk-Steno to Secretary, but we have to bid on the staff member we wish to work for. Two positions are now open for bid. The one I think I want is secretary to a man I've enjoyed working with in my present Air Traffic Division. It's a one-grade promotion. The other is secretary to the Sector Manager of the Airway Facilities Division (same building) and is a two-grade promotion. But I've heard rumors from reliable sources that I wouldn't want to work in the other division, for some valid-sounding reasons.

The job with the greater salary would be the obvious choice, but what if the rumors are true? My conflicting thoughts prompt me to bid on both jobs, though I'm hoping to stay in my present division. I feel more comfortable with what I know. Either way, I'll reach my goal of being a secretary, a dream coming true. I'm on pins and needles waiting for the announcement.

~

Oh boy, I've been selected for the job with Airway Facilities. God might have intervened, but I wonder what I've gotten myself into. I find out right away that my boss is a challenge to work for and I feel intimidated by him. I am relieved to soon discover that the other rumors I've heard are groundless, and I like the other people and the work itself. So it's not all that bad. My boss and I adjust to each other in time, but I'm rarely at ease in my situation. After a year or so, he retires early, due to a heart attack and bypass surgery.

To be honest, when I first heard of his heart attack, I instantly felt relief. Later on I realized that I wasn't feeling the sympathy and compassion I should be showing to him. He was going to have a lot of physical and emotional challenges to face as his life instantly changed, and here I was focused more on me than on him and his family. Not proud of that fact, I asked the Lord to forgive me and improve my attitude.

I guess God answered my prayer, when one of the staff members offered to take me to the hospital to visit him. It was a little awkward at first, but the visit was amiable and I'm glad I went. I never would have gone by myself.

It's a few months later now, and I'm working for a temporary boss until the new manager is selected. As I look up from my desk, there stands my former boss holding a schoolhouse pendulum clock. He's looking much healthier and very relaxed. I am in a pleasant state of shock when he presents me with this gift he made just for me! The precision of his talent as a clock-maker impresses me; it's a work of art. How about that!

A few years later, Mom and I drive down to his house when there's a problem with one of the clock parts. We have a very nice visit with him and his wife, and I learn that you don't really know what's going on under the surface of a person's exterior. Retirement is good for him, I can tell, and for the first time, I can see who the man really is. Perhaps the Lord changed his heart through his experience also. The beautiful clock still hangs on my dining room wall today.

In my sometimes-weird thinking, I wonder if God *caused* his heart attack-induced early retirement for *my* benefit, to give me a different boss (an audacious thought!), or for *his* benefit to leave the stress of the workplace, and to change some of his unhealthy habits. When I come to my senses later, I conclude that the Lord *knew* what would happen, and perhaps used this event to draw my boss into a closer relationship with Him. There's a difference between God *knowing* and *causing*, I'm learning. But He did work this circumstance for my good in the long run.

*One thing I am sure of, is that being in this division is worth the discomfort I'd felt before the new Manager arrived. I also didn't know at the time that I'd have a boss who would change my life considerably.*

# A Blackout of Another Kind

## God's Timing and Protection, Again

*"All the days ordained for me were written in Your book before one of them came to be."* (Psalm 139:16b.)

### Summer 1978

It's been 12 years since I moved to Miami, so I'm thinking it would be fun to go back and visit some of my New York friends. Mustering up some courage, I decide to take a vacation all by myself via Amtrak and stay with my friend Vinnie in Brooklyn. Our friendship that began with the orientation class at the Port Authority grew into a lasting one, so we still kept in touch occasionally through the years.

Riding Amtrak is a lot nicer than the subway, and though the reclining seat is comfortable, I know I won't sleep much during this 25-hour trip. It's much better than driving, though, and I hate to fly. I'm kind of apprehensive about who will be my seat-mate on this long ride, though.

A nice young girl who is traveling with her mother and brother plops down beside me, much to my relief. This friendly Christian family makes the trip fun. We play games with the kids and eat together in the dining car. It's nice to see the country this way, and as we pass through the Washington, D.C. area, I'm excited to see some of its landmarks. I have to say that I'm proud of myself for taking on this adventurous trip out of my usual comfort zone.

Vinnie meets me at the Amtrak station and we ride the subway from there to her house. I'm surprised at the improvements in the subway cars from 12 years ago. The cars are air conditioned now. What a change from the smelly, damp air I endured in my daily ride in the 1960's! The dingy seats have been replaced with colorful, modern ones, so it's a lot brighter atmosphere.

I'm really tired, but very happy to see my friend. She's married now, and she and her husband make me feel right at home. We've had fun at Coney Island and just got back from a wonderful restaurant for that great authentic New York Italian cuisine. Yum!

One day Vinnie takes me to her office at the World Trade Center. The Port Authority occupies many floors of this impressive skyscraper that I'd seen in the planning stage, many years ago. Her office is on the 72nd floor. We go there first. It's awesome to see the other tower through the wall of windows. I can hardly believe my eyes when I actually see it sway slightly; this is an amazing part of its engineering.

While the view is great, I wouldn't like working so high up. My office in the old Port Authority building was on the eleventh floor, and the cafeteria was on the 18th. I didn't even like that very well. Who knows what floor I'd be on, if I was still working for the P.A.

Now we take the express elevator to the observation floor at the very top. This elevator is the size of a small room. It feels like a plane ride and I think my ears popped. I hold on to the railing for dear life

The view from the top is breathtaking and worth the somewhat scary elevator ride. The glass walls on the observation floor give a wonderful 360-degree view of the city. There are window etchings identifying the bridges and buildings you see through them. It's thrilling to see the Statue of Liberty in the distance. As I look down, the people appear microscopic; it's *extremely* high. I don't stand too close because of my fear of heights, but I do take some pictures. You also get a close-up view of the smog that's not apparent from the ground. But I guess the Chamber of Commerce doesn't advertise that part. At least it was a clear enough day so I could see everything.

The express elevator down from the very top gives me quite a shock: when it stops on the ground floor, it feels like we're lifting back up at a high rate of speed for a few seconds. My stomach has been doing summersaults. I have to pry my fingers off the railing I've been gripping for the past minute and a half.

I'm very impressed with this building, but glad I don't work here. Most people don't have private offices. Vinnie's cubicle is one of probably 20 or 30, in an immense room. Everything is so BIG! To me, a nice cozy office like mine is a lot better.

The city is very crowded and everyone is in a hurry. (My friends in Miami are amused at how fast I walk; guess that New York quick-step has never left me.) People everywhere are focused only on their own agenda, eyes straight ahead to their next destination. The contrast between New York and Florida is mind-boggling to me now. New York's an interesting place to visit, but now I'm even more thankful that Dad moved us down south! Vinnie seems very happy there, though. I don't think she's lived anywhere else.

# September 11, 2001

Fast-forward to that date forever etched in history. I am still happily living in Florida and loving my job. The routine beginning hours of my workday are suddenly shattered when one of my co-workers comes running down the hall to the front office, barely able to speak.

"A plane just hit the World Trade Center, come quick," he sputters.

We rush into the break room and see replays of the passenger jet attacking the first tower and then watch live, in horror, as the second plane approaches and hits. We're all numb with disbelief as we hear that it's terrorist attacks, and I struggle to breathe when the second tower implodes. I am almost paralyzed with fear. The terror before my eyes and the unknown hits me especially hard when I quickly realize I could have been working there if we hadn't moved.

It's apparent that this attack isn't over, so my boss activates the FAA's emergency plan, and sends me home. The air traffic controllers, supervisors and staff are on high alert and landing remaining flights before all air traffic ceases. This is one time I'm glad to be called a "non-essential" employee. My workplace is in lockdown after I leave.

At home, I'm glued to the TV. Though too graphically painful to watch, I'm drawn like a magnet. Such familiar scenes of my earlier years in Manhattan make this horrendous event uncomfortably personal. At age 54 now, I probably would have still been working for the Port Authority. After working there for just a year, I could see the potential of it being a great career for me.

My mind is now tuned to a song on my Twila Paris CD. I play "God is in Control" and my panic level recedes, hearing the truth in those words. Yet I worry, will our country be in all-out war? What's going to happen next? Am I safe anywhere?

I'm heart-broken for the victims and their loved ones, and pray for them. I think of my friend Vinnie and a few days later contact her. Thank God, she'd recently changed careers and is teaching at a school in Brooklyn now. She's upset, of course, but grateful she wasn't near Ground Zero, and that no one dear to her was in the building that fateful day.

I send Vinnie some of the photos I took from the top of the WTC in 1978. They were faded with age, but she was very grateful to have them. She had never taken any pictures.

*Did God intervene to move me out of harm's way? I believe that's one of the reasons He moved our family to Florida. Only God knows what could have been. As the shock ebbs to a manageable level, I thank God that I wasn't there, and also for His other definite protections in my life.*

*I'm grateful that I was no longer exposed to the many dangerous situations in New York occurring over the years. The year after I graduated, I was told there were swat teams regularly patrolling each floor of my high school, due to increased crime. Gang activity was everywhere and I heard that our formerly safe neighborhood was becoming crime-ridden also. Again, God's intervention in the form of protection.*

> *But I have digressed from my story of God's continuous hand in the 1960's. This time it's in my spiritual life*

# Spiritual and Church Awakenings

## God Reveals Himself, and the Church as It's Meant to Be

*"For it is by grace you have been saved, through faith – and that not of yourselves, it is the gift of God."* (Ephesians 2:8a.)

*"And God raised us up with Christ and seated us with Him."* (Ephesians 2:6a)

### Growing Up in New York

Our small church (which my grandfather physically built) is all I've known since birth. I think its beliefs are pretty rigid, but I can tell that the people of our congregation of 80 or so love Jesus. The general message I have *felt* and continue to *feel* is short on demonstrating and preaching grace, and long on keeping rules and judging. While the sermons aren't as severe as the "hell fire and damnation" ones I occasionally hear from visiting evangelists, I still feel under pressure at church more times than not. I've discovered in the last few years that this is called legalism.

At school, I feel like an odd-ball, because there are so many things I'm not allowed to do. There are very few evangelical Protestants like me in New York's mixing pot of all races and religions. Even most of the Protestant kids in my classes don't have our denominational restrictions (at the time) against dancing, going to the movies, playing cards, and not doing anything on Sunday besides going to church - just to name a few. I really don't understand why the church is so unyielding about these things. I love Jesus but am bothered by all these restrictions.

Because Mom and Dad are compliant with the rules in the church manual, I have always refrained from participating in those areas, obedient daughter that I am. That's not to say I haven't occasionally questioned Mom, who is the most verbal of my parents in spiritual matters.

There were a few times when I nagged and whined, enveloped in my distress at feeling so odd in comparison to the school society I wanted so desperately to fit into. Mom pushed aside my questions with vague answers, and never relented despite my attempts to force the issue. It seemed to me that she wasn't sure why these things were taboo, but didn't want to rock the boat. I feel uncertainty emanating from her and Dad in these matters.

This problem came to a head when the three of us agonized over a social dancing class that I was required to take in Junior High as part of Phys. Ed. Mom and Dad finally gave in and let me take the course, which was above-board and very properly taught. To this day I fail to understand how people would think God would be offended by the class. At least I was very relieved to not be further seen as a social misfit. Of course, I didn't go to the senior prom a few years later, because no one asked me, and I doubt my parents would have let me go anyway! They're pretty strict, but never harsh with me. I think they feel trapped but won't admit it. The rigidity I feel is from the church, not them.

$\sim$

For too many years, I have felt that life is a bunch of "should not's" and "must's," and that God is up in Heaven with a baseball bat, watching to see if I mess up. I know Mom and Dad don't believe that consciously, but I sense a hidden fear in them, a "what will people (or God) think of us" mindset.

This does nothing to help my conflicting thoughts of being afraid of God, and yet believing He loves me. I feel that being a Christian is mostly a dismal bunch of rules and a lot of effort on my part. I don't think I understand grace fully. I read the Bible religiously but still don't quite "get it."

To be fair, I have to admit that I have seen the love of Jesus during many of our church services over the years. I also remember times when everyone was worshipping in the Spirit with heart-felt tears, just enjoying God's presence, and how people would share how the Lord helped them through crises. But those times just break up the judging atmosphere I feel.

I am not against church or my denomination. I am forever grateful for my Christian heritage and for my church. It's just that there's some kind of conflict that I feel spiritually, and I don't know what to do about it.

*It's taken many years for me to stop blaming my parents for these underlying fears and spiritual confusion. Now I understand that they were raised in that kind of environment, too. This pervasive spiritual rigidity seemed to be especially prevalent in certain parts of the country during my growing-up years. I know it still exists in some places.*

# A Spiritual Metamorphosis in Miami

## July 1966

Right from the first church service I attend in Miami, I can feel God's presence, and how His Spirit moves on so many of the people of the congregation. There's a spirit of freedom and joy in this place that is contagious! Miami Central (same denomination) is larger than our New York church, with about 350 people each Sunday. The love of the Lord is obvious to me as the people so passionately love Jesus and care for each other. Our pastor is a wonderful, lively, loving man of God. He lets his hair down, so to speak, coming down to our level. He's funny but reverent at the same time. To me, he is an illustration of uninhibited freedom in Christ.

To my surprise, I immediately feel at home with the people of this wonderful church. That alone is God's intervention, because of my inborn shyness and resistance to change. It's amazing to see people's lives changed, sometimes right before your eyes. There are times before or after the services when a few people will spontaneously go into another room to pray. God is alive here! I can feel the power of God moving among us.

After a church service emphasizing baptism, I wonder why I've never been baptized. As we start dinner, I ask,

"Mom, have you ever been baptized?"

"Yes, when I was in my 20's. Why do you ask?"

"Well, why haven't I been baptized? I know I was dedicated as a baby, but this is different, isn't it?"

"Yes, it's by choice and profession of faith. We didn't have a baptistry in our Richmond Hill church. It really wasn't practical to baptize there; you'd have to travel to a river pretty far from the church."

I guess Dad and Judy catch my desire to participate in this sacrament, so one special Sunday evening, the three of us are baptized. I still remember climbing Miami Central's somewhat rickety steps to the baptistry high above the choir loft, despite my fear of heights and of being dunked. Though I'm very uncomfortable and self-conscious, as I come up out of the water, I sense God's presence. I feel so clean and make a renewed confession of my faith in Jesus. This is such a wonderful memory, that I will always cherish.

Soon our family gets involved in not just the church, but in finding a ministry that God wants to use us in. Mom starts a neighborhood Bible study in our home. The interaction with other people's perspectives on truths that never change help me personalize the Bible better. Dad is supportive of this ministry, but pretty quiet during the meetings. I begin to learn that words are only one way of demonstrating Christ. My Dad is a godly man.

Judy leads a teen Bible study at our home a few years later. Her closeness to the Lord through these Bible study times is part of the foundation which will sustain her later on, through a story that's only hers to tell.

I am relieved to learn that the Holy Spirit is a gift sent from God to all believers. God's love for me and His amazing grace begin to motivate me to do what pleases Him. Instead of keeping rules in my own strength and out of guilt, I realize that serving God comes from my heart, in response to all He has done for me.

Though love and grace are continuous themes of this Miami church, God's standards for holy living are not watered down from His written Word. I learn that the gray areas not spelled out in the Bible are worked out through personal convictions in the heart and mind of each individual person. The church can be a guide, but the Lord is the judge.

# The Church Library

For a few years, I don't feel a specific calling from God to do anything for Him, preferring to just get through each day, which is busy enough with my full-time job. But one day Mom is asked to organize the books that Miami Central has collected over the years, and establish a real library. She agrees with enthusiasm, not having a clue how to go about it. She purchases a library starter kit from our denomination's publishing house and dives right in.

This interests me because I love to read books. Mom used to call me a 'bookworm' and push me out of the house when I'd have my nose in a book all day long. I'm now helping her catalog books by hand (this is before computers), and put in book pockets and check-out cards. We also type title, author and subject cards. I am comfortable with this kind of behind-the-scenes work, though I see it as more of a job than a calling. Finally we're finished, and ready to offer all sorts of reading opportunities to the people of our congregation. At least the library work isn't a time-consuming project all of the time.

Mom and I staff the Library before and after Sunday School, offering spiritual growth books, Christian fiction, Bible study helps, biographies and other inspirational books. People come in to chat and sometimes share prayer requests. I'm beginning to see that this is more than just a display of books. I'm catching Mom's vision a little, I think. I guess I can see this as a joint ministry for both Mom and me. Is this all God wants me to do for Him right now?

As I read Ephesians 2:6, something leaped out at me: It says we are seated with Jesus Christ. That means we can rest in Him. I'm learning that the less complicated my thoughts are, the closer I come to the simple truth of the Gospel. Whatever else God has for me to do, He will work it out.

I consider these revelations as Divine intervention from God, as the Holy Spirit guides me and helps me nail down my beliefs. Perhaps this move from New York was part of God's plan for me to get to know Him better. What a foundation to help me later on as my life will face increasingly difficult challenges.

# My Social Life Takes Off

## God Gradually Pulls Me Out of My Shell

*"Forget the former things; do not dwell on the past. See, I am doing a new thing! Now is springs up; do you not perceive it? I am making a way in the desert and streams in the wasteland."* (Isaiah 43:18-19.)

New York
1965-1966

In my earlier years, our church had a slightly larger congregation, with a wonderful children's ministry. I fondly remember Vacation Bible School and "Caravan" (our denomination's equivalent to Girl Scouts). Even these activities were hard for me in the beginning because of my extreme shyness; Mom would sometimes have to push me out the door. But I eventually got the hang of it and learned to enjoy these events.

Our congregation shrunk through the years, but we still have a great youth group of various ages. On Friday nights, we get together at "Pals." The eight or ten of us teens and pre-teens play Ping-Pong and other games in the church basement. We occasionally go out to wholesome entertaining events. At least I have this social outlet, because I sure don't at school. Well, except for football games and the few girlfriends I occasionally do stuff with.

I think I've been virtually ignored by guys at school because I look (and probably act) much younger than my age. Being shy and tiny is probably a factor. At the New York World's Fair in 1964, I was asked at the ticket booth if I was over 12 (I was 17 at the time!) I was highly offended! This did nothing for my self-image. When will boys ever start to notice me?

I have to admit, though, that I've been growing a little as a person *now,* as I've adjusted to the working world. My friendships there have helped improve my self-concept. I was excited to attend a baseball game at newly opened Shea Stadium with Vinnie and another of my work friends. They live in Brooklyn, so we arranged to meet at a station between our opposite subway routes. This was challenging for me, as I had to travel alone part of the way. Fortunately, we found each other quickly, at the arranged time. I was proud of myself for taking on this new-to-me adventure.

We watched the Los Angeles (formerly Brooklyn) Dodgers play the NY Mets. Don't remember who won, but who cares? To us, they were both New York teams. New Yorkers are fanatic baseball fans and the game was high-pitched excitement (pun intended). We had a lot of fun and were like excitable teeny-boppers as we gazed dreamily through the fence at some of the players, on our way out.

~

As spring of 1966 now emerges and brings with it a small dose of spring fever to me, I start to feel tingles down my arm when my church's 27-year-old youth leader helps me on with my light coat. We've known each other pretty well in this small congregation, but I sense something a little more personal in this brief moment. I wonder if it's my imagination. He hasn't dated much that I'm aware of, and I know he isn't dating anyone right now.

Now that I'm almost 19, I suddenly realize that the nine-year age gap doesn't matter so much to me. Something in his glance makes me think that he's starting to see me a little differently; know what I mean? He's just bought a new convertible and I am now riding in the front seat with him as we're going with the "Pals" group to a baseball game. Spring's gentle breeze flowing through my hair fills up my senses. My romantic imagination is probably reading more into this than reality, especially with several other people in the car with us. It is a group event, after all.

But shortly after that, he plans a group skiing trip to upstate New York; and he *personally* talks me into going. I've never been on skis and am not at all athletic or coordinated, but I guess his encouragement persuades me to sign up. He even offers to pick me up from work, which really has me thinking more and more about him. I tell my co-worker and she's excited for me.

Though one part of me really, really wants to go, my fear of skiing for the first time wins out. I'm afraid I'll break my leg or something. Phys. Ed was my only mediocre subject in school. So I actually decide to back out. (My co-worker thinks I'm crazy to pass up this fun and possibly romantic event.)

I can see that he's really disappointed when I tell him I'm not going. Maybe he's more than a little disappointed? And not just because he's my youth leader? As I continue to wonder, I sometimes dream about him. Did I make a mistake in canceling?

Whatever might be starting to happen between us is abruptly cut short when the time to move to Florida suddenly arrives. I'll probably never know what might have been....or will I?

~

At work, my friends take me out for a farewell lunch. They surprise me with a beautiful watch pendant and a loving card. Having known them for only a year, I feel important and special at this parting gift, and I realize that these social interactions have been beginning steps in my becoming more outgoing and independent. I really don't want to be a wallflower!

The people in my department throw me a small party and give me gifts, though I've only worked in that office for a few months. I'm surprised at the affection they've shown me. Am I blind to being liked by people, only seeing my own imperfections? Why else would I be so surprised? I think I have a lot to learn.

# A Happy New Start in Miami

## 1966-1969

It's the second Sunday of July, 1966. I already know inside of me that this move is better for me socially than I ever expected. The church has a large College and Career Sunday School class with lots of activities. I feel pleased at how warmly I'm welcomed into the class. I'm a little embarrassed when they all tease me about my New York accent; especially those true Southern Belles from the Deep South! But I can tell that it really is good-natured affection.

I do manage to lose my accent in record time, just by being around them, I guess. While on vacation later on, I'm at a restaurant in the Florida Panhandle with my parents. The 'Florida Cracker' accent of the waitress is too much for Mom and Dad, so I have to translate – both ways! Their 'Noo Yawk' accents never leave; guess I'm young enough to take on a new one. (Twelve years later my New York friends said that I have a *southern* accent!)

The church service is beginning, and my heart starts to pound a little as I am mesmerized, watching an unbelievably gorgeous blonde with a Florida tan play the organ beautifully and soulfully. He's about my age, home from college for the summer. I can hardly believe it when I ask around and find out he isn't dating anyone. He's pleasant to me when we happen to be around each other at the class's social events, but only from a distance. My fantasy bubble is quickly deflated, as I find out that looks aren't everything.

The social events are frequent and fun, and I am so happy to be accepted just exactly as I am by these people who are my peers. This is a contrast from New York, where I was basically ignored at school. At my New York church, the Pals group dwindled to just a few after

I graduated, and those remaining were a lot younger than me. Well, except for the youth leader who I was just beginning to know better.

Here in Miami there are actually guys my age, and after awhile I do have a few dates. But nothing lasts. I wonder if it's me. Am I not attractive enough, or what? Over the next two or three years, most of our group find their soul mates at the out-of-state colleges they attend. Our singles class has dropped to just a few gals, and my romantic prospects are fading away.

My social life picks up again when Dianne, a nursing student, returns to Miami to begin her career at Hialeah Hospital. She's the daughter of one of Mom's new church friends, and we soon become good friends also. We have fun on weekends, take several vacations together and go on a few cruises to the Bahamas. It's great to have a girlfriend, but something's missing – in one word, guys!

I've just bought my brand new Chevelle Malibu and Dianne has just showed up at church in her new Mustang. All of a sudden we have the attention of two cute guys, and we take them for rides in our new cars. They are a few years younger than us, have their licenses but no cars yet. The four of us become good friends.

In the evenings, we ride aimlessly but happily around town and to the beaches, just to have something to do. We let them drive and take turns at the wheel, alternating cars on the different nights we go out. They like to talk and we have lots of laughs, and a lot of good, clean fun. Although we did have one unexpected encounter with the law:

We're just about to switch drivers and are parked on a side street in North Miami for a few minutes, just talking (yes, really!). It is way past midnight and I'm startled when a police officer suddenly appears at my car window! I didn't see that coming!

"What are you doing?" he asks, as I pull out my license and registration.

"We're switching drivers and on our way back home." I hope he doesn't notice how nervous I am.

"You can't just park here, better get moving."

Fortunately, he believes our explanation, and we take off quickly, thankful he didn't give us a ticket – or a car search (not that we were hiding anything). *Those are my only 'wild days' of staying out way past midnight; think I've led a sheltered life?*

I know that our guy friends like us for our cars, but we still have a lot of fun – the classic 'just friends' status, maybe because we're older. At this point, I think age matters; they're still in high school!

*I really think this move to Miami was part of God's intervention to help me blossom as a young woman. I am gradually emerging out of this cocoon I've woven around myself since childhood. I'm still shy, but maybe this social interaction with my peers would have taken a lot longer back in New York. I'm so very happy to have Christian friends my age.*

# The Accident I Can't Remember

## God's Provision and Protection

*"Because he loves Me," says the Lord, I will rescue him; I will protect him, for he acknowledges My name. He will call upon Me and I will answer him; I will be with him in trouble, I will deliver him and honor him. With long life I will satisfy him and show him my salvation."* (Psalm 91:14-16.)

A Crash and a Save
November 1974
Miami, Florida

I've been driving for about seven years now, but as the population of Hialeah and Miami has grown by leaps and bounds, the busier, hectic traffic and bad drivers have gotten on my nerves. In New York we used public transportation most of the time, except for going to church or visiting friends and relatives. So you could say that driving a car hasn't been a dominant way of life for my family until now, and I only drive to get places, not for fun anymore. But I believe I am a very safe driver, maybe more careful than most.

On Saturdays, our church has a ministry to visit families of the children who ride the Sunday School bus. Mom and I usually go together, but this time it's just her best friend Frieda and me. We've finished our route now and I'm driving her home in my 1968 red-with-black-interior Chevelle Malibu. I really like this car; it has never given me any trouble from the day I bought it new, and I think it looks really cool with its new paint job. The Florida sun fades paint, so it was time, and I decided to change the color from yellow to cherry red. We're not far from Frieda's home. It's a quiet street, with little traffic.

**For an instant, I'm aware of a flash of blinding sunlight and blue sky, complete silence, then nothing.**

The next memory I have is waking up in the Emergency Room, and notice a church family friend by my side. I hear him excitedly call Mom over; "Betty's back," he says. Mom asks me, "Do you know where you are, and what happened?" By then I realize, with a dull thud, that I'm in a hospital and conclude that I've had an accident. My mind is still slowed down to a snail's pace and I don't want to be bothered by the details. In fact, I don't feel like thinking at all. I just want to sink back into oblivion.

Mom tells me I've been talking non-stop, and while making sense to those who don't know me, Mom is certain that something is very wrong. She says my personality has been very different over the past seven hours, and I've been saying and doing things completely out of character. Of course, I don't remember any of this. I'm glad she doesn't get specific with the details, or I'd be in a constant state of embarrassment! Mom's relieved that at least I'm partially 'back.'

The doctor says I have a severe concussion. I'm also told that I had plastic surgery on my ear, which had split in two when I fell over my half-open car window. I also have a broken clavicle. I'm very uncomfortable, and for several days I can't even get up to use the bathroom. It's a helpless feeling, not to mention the indignity of using a bedpan. But I can't say it bothers me that much. I'm kind of in a state of nothingness. My hospital room-mate isn't very friendly, but I don't feel like talking anyway.

When I feel good enough to handle exactly what happened, Mom relays the following account, told to her by Frieda (who has a slight concussion and minor injuries). Mom seems to be re-living this accident vicariously for me as she speaks.

*Apparently distracted, I don't stop or slow down enough at a yield sign to avoid crashing into a speeding vehicle which has the right of way. My car spins around wildly as Frieda and I are knocked unconscious. I miss crashing into a telephone pole by a few inches, and then the hedges on someone's front yard stop my out-of-control car. After a few minutes, the roaring motor jolts and revives Frieda enough to lean over and turn off the ignition.*

*An off-duty paramedic runs to the scene and holds my heavily bleeding, severed ear together with pressure and towels until the ambulance arrives. I keep asking him, "Am I going to die?" and when he says that I'm fine, and no, I'm not going to die, I weakly say, "Praise the Lord!" This constant back-and-forth identical conversation continues right up to the arrival of the ambulance. When they roll me into the emergency vehicle, I aggressively grab the hand of the African-American male attendant and hold it throughout the ride to the hospital. (Who is this person? Not me, surely!) I'm later told what a kind, compassionate man he was to me.*

*Also at the scene, I am issued a ticket for causing the accident. The police officer apologizes for having to do this, and asks Frieda to give it to me when I'm feeling better. (Of course, I'm unaware of this at the time.)*

*I have plastic surgery on my left ear, and because I've broken the clavicle on my right side, they elect to put me in a figure 8 brace, so that I don't have to heal from surgery on both sides of my body. I have no recollection of any of this, and don't think I needed anesthesia, because I was feeling no pain!*

# Getting Back Together Again

My patched-up ear looks so beautiful, other doctors and nurses come in to see the extraordinary work of the plastic surgeon. They take 'before and after' pictures. I'm a celebrity! I find this amusing; I haven't felt the full impact of what happened yet.

I've mostly emerged from "la la land," though I've had some pretty embarrassing moments in the hospital, best left unsaid. Thankfully, my brain gradually returns to normal, but they keep me in the hospital for a week. I'm still woozy until my day of discharge.

Mom tells me later that the worker where my car was impounded said that no one should have survived such a horrible crash. God proved him wrong! However, the effect the sight of my badly-mangled, totaled car had on Mom, when she and Dad went to retrieve my personal items, made her wish she hadn't seen it. Dad took whatever was in the glove compartment; she would have just left in shock. Mom seems more upset by my accident than I am. But then again, I'm not on all four burners yet.

I'm happily surprised that my insurance pays full blue book value for my recently repainted car. It still had low mileage and had been in great mechanical shape. I kind of grieve over losing this car that I liked so much. After I recover, I buy a brand new Dodge Dart, in sea-foam green. To this day, I will not buy a red vehicle.

The day has come to show up at traffic court. I have been dreading this. Though Mom takes me, I'm really scared and still traumatized. I see the driver of the other car for the first time and notice he is wearing a neck brace. "Oh great" I think. While waiting for my case to come up, I watch the judge as he deals with each of the defendants; my nerves increasing incrementally with each one. He gets tough with some of the cases, but seems fair and nice enough if you get on his good side.

As I continue to wait, I debate whether I should plead "guilty with an explanation" because the skid marks indicated the other driver was speeding, or say "guilty" and get it over with. "Guilty" is all that comes out of my mouth. The judge, in his mercy, only fines me a small amount for failure to yield right of way. God has helped me through yet another difficult situation. I breathe a sigh of relief.

My nerves are set on edge again when the property owners whose front yard my car damaged sue me. I've never been sued before! Panic sets in, but then I remember to contact my insurance company, and that's the end of it. Wow, what a relief! Thankfully, I have no problems with the driver with the neck brace. It would be interesting to know what he got out of his insurance payout. When my insurance premium comes due at its regular time, I breathe a sigh of relief. They didn't drop me; another miracle!

Because I work for the government, I have good sick leave, and can recuperate at home for two and a half months. The healing is slow, but permanent. I've put off driving, but know I have to get behind the wheel again to conquer my fear. After a few times, it gets easier.

I finally decide to go back to the accident scene with Mom. I'm wondering if anything would come back, but nothing does. I guess I felt that I had to go there, for some closure. I also wanted to thank the neighborhood paramedic who helped me, but he wasn't home.

How thankful I am that God protected me and that my injuries were not more serious. I came to realize that God still protects, even when I am careless or distracted. I believe God protected me from crashing into the telephone pole, a possible death sentence. The paramedic was at the right place at the right time, to save my ear. I don't believe that was a coincidence.

God's mercy kept me from having to relive the accident that I don't remember. Those seven hours remain lost, and I've never had flashbacks.

I realized later that because I was praising the Lord at the accident scene, my faith was stronger than I was aware of. I would need a stronger faith before long, to get me through some new experiences and choices I would have to make.

# Workplace Challenges
# and Temptations

## Moving with God into Unfamiliar Territory

*"No temptation has seized you except what is common to man. And God is faithful; He will not let you be tempted beyond what you can bear. But when you are tempted, He will also provide a way out so that you can stand up under it."* (I Cor. 10:13).

FAA Airway Facilities Division
Miami ARTCC
1972 - 1980

I'm now working for my new boss as an Executive Secretary, GS-6. I find myself quickly challenged with some new experiences as he takes over. He's only been here a few days when he asks me to attend and take minutes at a meeting of 22 supervisors and staff. This is something I've never done before and I don't have a clue how to go about it. I feel panic building, but somehow I get through it.

These frequent meetings get a little easier each time. I learn that they repeat themselves a lot, which helps if I miss something. Summarizing what they mean can be confusing and a challenge when they have trouble getting to the point. Amazingly, later on I become quite comfortable with this, and at times wish I could speak up and tell those with opposing views to really listen to each other! From what I've observed, most meetings are a waste of time, but it does give me practice with my shorthand.

I'm getting used to many new aspects of my job, and am relieved that the boss-secretary function is beginning to flow easily and smoothly. We're a real team, and I find myself eagerly looking forward to going to work each day. This boss is the best one I've ever had!

I feel like a queen when my own private office is modernized with new furniture, drapes and carpet, which I happily get to pick out. This is so much more than I ever expected. I'm really moving up in this world, and loving it!

# Uh, Oh

All of a sudden my comfortable world is rocked when my boss enthusiastically informs me that I'm going to attend a 4-day secretarial conference for the whole Southern Region in Atlanta, Georgia. This is the first time they've ever held one, and it's highly supported by management.

Enthusiasm is not *my* word for this news! I'm still in my 20's, and don't want to fly by myself (I'm terrified of flying!) I've never stayed in a hotel alone and that's scary for me, too. I try every excuse I can think of to get out of it, but my boss won't take no for an answer. Because the conference is only for Airway Facilities secretaries, I'm the only one going from my building. I am dreading this and praying a lot.

I hope for an easy flight, but the plane trip starts with an hour-long weather hold on the taxiway. We're in a long line of planes waiting to take off, and my nerve-based adrenalin increases with each passing minute. Let's just get this over with!

Finally we take off, still in a thunderstorm, as I see lightning through the window. What are we doing, flying in a storm? Though my nerves are still giving me fits, it comforts me that I'm sitting next to a priest. I'm disappointed that he's not talkative, but I figure God's got us covered. A huge air pocket drops the plane suddenly, along with my stomach. Nobody but me seems disturbed, so I calm down some.

We finally land safely and somehow I find my way to the hotel. I am relieved to meet some other secretaries right away. The first night in my private hotel room isn't as bad as I feared, and Mom helps me calm down some more when I phone home. I manage to get a little sleep, probably from mental exhaustion.

~

The four-day conference is partly familiarization with Regional Headquarters and partly training to help offices operate uniformly. In spite of my state of agitation, I do learn a few things that are useful in my job, and it's nice to have a picture in my mind now of many of the people I coordinate with on the phone.

I meet two friendly ladies to go out to eat with, so their company keeps me from feeling too lonely. By the second day I'm feeling better and calm down a bit. The conference leaders are very nice and make each of us feel very important and valued. On our last evening they take all of us to Stone Mountain Park for dinner. That was a big treat and probably the highlight of my trip.

Well, I guess it all turned out okay, but I'm so happy to be back home! It's fun typing my own travel voucher when I get back, and being paid per diem! But I wouldn't want to do this ever, ever again.

*God didn't intervene by giving me an "out," but I think He helped me through the Atlanta trip and conference just to show me He could. Traveling as a routine part of my job wasn't in His plans, though, for which I was very thankful. It was the first and only secretarial conference that I know of.*

# You Want Me to Do What?

I'm relieved to have that behind me, and am looking forward to getting back to the routine now. Not so! I'm shocked to learn that the trip was just the beginning of more 'flights' out of my comfort zone. Not wasting any time, my boss introduces me to the first of many social events I have to plan and attend as part of my job.

My boss has now given me the job of organizing, attending and collecting money at an executive board luncheon for managers of various federal agencies in the greater Miami area. I've never done anything like this and have butterflies in my stomach as that day approaches. I feel intimidated among all these VIP's, but actually I do fine and am pleased by the respectful friendliness they show me. It's an amazing thought to me that I'm treated as an equal, and not a servant.

I'm not used to such ritzy surroundings with high-end menus. It is kind of like that New York glitz I'd had a taste of years ago. The food is very good, and the atmosphere and service are first class. My boss covers my meal, of course.

These luncheons meet monthly and progress to other work-related gatherings (during office hours) which I have to plan and attend. Sometimes we meet in expensive restaurants or hotel conference rooms. This is an expected part of my job now. There are usually only about 20 people at most of these more formal meetings, but that's more than I feel very comfortable with. Everything is very classy; my boss transferred from Washington Headquarters and brought a lot of that kind of sophistication with him. Despite my discomfort, I'm relieved to pull off these events successfully. I start feeling like I'm being treated royally, and think maybe I could get used to this.

Over the period of a few years, I've now become more an Office Manager and Administrative Assistant than the classic definition of a secretary. My boss occasionally involves me in some of his decisions that extend beyond mere office management. At times I feel like the Assistant Airway Facilities Manager. Though I feel my self-esteem slowly growing, I think it's mostly confined to work-related confidence. I still feel insecure outside of work.

# Not Again!

Why can't my job just stay where I can breathe easily? Now my boss is again stretching the lines of my comfort zone: I have to plan and attend a really big retirement party for one of our employees. We have a workforce of over 100 people, and most bring their spouses to this kind of evening event.

I feel very out of place around the majority of people who drink cocktails, some quite freely, and sometimes there's dancing (which I never pursued since Jr. High). Raised so strictly against these church-defined vices, I feel like a square peg in a round hole. There's a social sophistication I don't fit into, and I don't like being in large gatherings, either. At least I don't have to emcee or make a speech, and can stay in the background. I wish I didn't have to go to these things!

To add to my discomfort, I always have to go alone, being spouseless and dateless. Except once.

I imagine myself arriving at the latest event with an actual date, and how good that would make me feel. "Why not make this a reality?" I ask myself. So one Sunday at church I pitifully ask a very good-looking friend from my past (the one I drove around with in the 1960's) to escort me.

"Would you please help me out with a problem I have?" I start out.

He looks pretty approachable and interested.

"I have to attend an evening retirement party and hate going to these mandatory work events alone. Would you be willing to go with me?"

He just stares into space. I can't read his face. The suspense is killing me. I actually reduce myself to begging. I tell him how uncomfortable it is for me and how bad I feel at never having a date.

(Actually I still like him after all these years, but he doesn't see me as more than a casual friend.)

"OK."

Not an enthusiastic response, but I'll take it, along with a huge sigh of relief. I'm glad I didn't embarrass myself for nothing.

When we arrive, he offers me his arm, which I hold onto, pretending we're 'an item.' I suddenly have the attention of a lot of my co-workers. Now *that* has everyone talking! They want to know where I've been hiding him. It is a great feeling to have him there with me, and we catch up on some events of our lives. I think he enjoys himself, too. When he drives me home, we sit in the car and talk for a long time, just like old times way back when.

But I can't lie; I have to confess to my co-workers later on that he is only a friend. Well, at least I survive each of those gala events and pull them off. Everyone seems to have a good time there, in spite of my negative feelings.

God intervened in these work-related socially challenging situations by not getting me out of what I naturally did not wish to do. Though I don't know why I was put in these uncomfortable events, I do believe it was part of a growth process, as I was slowly learning how to relate to people different from me. I'm still learning.

# Temptation

I'm thankful to not be unduly pressured into doing anything against my religious convictions at work or socially, though occasionally some people do try to persuade me. It's when tempting opportunities come to mind that I question some of the church's standards, as I rethink my own. Most of the time I have it figured out. Until now.

A specific temptation has been following me around for months. The time I spend outside of the sheltered environment I was raised in seems to dim God's voice a bit, and opens my mind to other viewpoints. Sometimes I just don't know how to respond to something that appears innocent but possibly isn't. This is one of those times. I now have conflicting, confused thoughts about this particular ongoing situation and relationship. So far I've chosen to ignore the caution flags in my mind, and have rationalized to myself what I've let continue on with this man – because I like it. I can't get very specific, but I need to vent.

*Maybe I just didn't even want to hear God's voice that clearly at first, but I believe God has been strongly intervening in my mind with His Word and through Mom's insightful comments these past few days. I've put off this decision because in my thinking, we haven't done anything sinful. But God revealed to me that in His eyes, this isn't innocent and is dangerous territory for me. I have to respond to what God has now made plain: that this aspect of my relationship with this man is not okay, because he's married. Period.*

*I'm in panic mode again as I consider what I have to do. No more excuses or delays. It's time. I'm a nervous wreck, but resolute. With God's grace, courage and even exact words, I face* the situation squarely, and then breathe a sigh of relief when it is accomplished. I'm so glad I made the right choice and didn't cross that line God Himself had drawn for me. I'd come dangerously close to making choices leading toward a downward spiral in some of my relationships and my own spiritual life.

~

There's some awkwardness for a short time, but everything turns out the way it should. In fact, several very good things happen later on, which are connected to this critical decision. I'm so thankful for God's help in doing what was right, and rescuing me from possible disaster.

*I still have lots to learn in following God's guidance through the tricky areas of living as a Christian where most people around me don't share my beliefs or my stricter moral standards.*

*There's a fine line between conviction and tolerance. Sometimes I've been told that I come across as judgmental or harsh. That certainly isn't my intent; in fact, if anything, I feel inferior and somewhat of a misfit. Maybe I've been focusing more on the 'do's and don'ts,' or what people think of me, than on being close to the Lord and enjoying His Presence.*

*It's God's Presence I'm going to need as I will soon have a very unnerving set of changing circumstances.*

# Mom's Tragedy
# and Triumphant Legacy

## God's 'Grace-full' Involvement in Every Detail

*"I know the plans I have for you," says the Lord,*
*"plans to prosper you and not to harm you, plans to give*
*you hope and a future."* (Jeremiah 29:11).

### Miami, Florida
### November 1976

It's late November, an ordinary sunny, pleasant autumn day; but a day I will never forget. Mom approaches me with a scared look on her face. She has found a lump in her breast, and she must know somehow that it's serious, from what I read on her countenance. Her emergency mammogram and doctor visit give us some hope. Dr. Johnson says there's a 95% chance it's benign. When she asks if the surgery can wait until after Christmas, the doctor agrees. I'm relieved and prepare to enjoy the holidays.

### January 1977

Mom is calm (Dad and I aren't) going into surgery. She won't know until she wakes up if the operation was "the big one" or just a lumpectomy. Mom doesn't want me to take off work, so every time the phone rings, my heart pounds in suspense as I wonder if it's the news I'm waiting and hoping for. Either Dad's forgotten to call, or the surgery is taking hours longer than expected. Finally the call comes.

"Bad news. The doctor says it is stage five cancer and doesn't look good. They've done a double mastectomy, and removed seven lymph glands. She's going to be in the hospital a long time. She's lost a lot of blood and is sleeping, not quite recovered from the anesthesia. The surgery took a very long time. They're planning multiple blood transfusions."

Dad sounds very tired and weary. My heart sinks.

"Oh, no. I'll be praying; that's all we can do right now, I guess. I'll come by after work." This doesn't seem real and I feel very numb. I stand against the wall and let my mind go blank. Then I tell my boss and he lets me go home early.

"Why, Lord, why?" I pray. Mom has always maintained a healthy lifestyle; I don't understand. My world comes crashing down. What are we going to do? Is she going to survive this? I pray continually, engulfed in "what if's." This is very scary for all of us.

Mom receives several blood transfusions during the 28 days she is hospitalized. Dr. Johnson makes the unusual decision to start the chemotherapy while she's still there, even though she's in an extremely weakened state. Mom already senses that this unusually caring doctor is a gift from God, and trusts his judgment. If we were still living in New York, I don't think she would have gotten such good care. He goes far beyond his call of duty, and constantly monitors her progress.

I believe Dr. Johnson actually loves my mother and has a special attachment to her. He doesn't appear to be close to the Lord, but tells Mom that her faith and positive attitude are greatly helping her overcome this disease. Her hospital roommate is a believer, and they encourage each other with their faith. Many prayers ascend to Heaven daily for her healing and recovery.

What can I do for her, besides pray? I search some of the promises in the Bible and type a card with the hope of Jeremiah 29:11. I try to feed that promise for her into my own spirit. What would I do without her? It's a scary thought to me, and I pray for God to spare her life for my own sake as well as hers and Dad's.

It's a happy day when Mom finally gets to come home, but she has a long road ahead of her - nine months of brutal chemotherapy. (Chemo in the 1970's was much worse than it is today.) After a few treatments she says she has to quit, the reaction to it is too horrible for words. But her strong will to live and her faith in God pull her through each time. In between chemo doses, Mom gains enough strength to face the next one.

# A Vacation that Turns Tragic, Then Miraculous

Getting away from everything sounds good to all of us, so after a few months, Mom, Dad and I drive to Texas for a short vacation to visit Mom's brother and family. She has the second, lower mid-month dose of chemo in Houston (as an outpatient). This dose is much lighter than the larger dose and treatment, and rarely causes her any major problems.

Late that evening, Mom becomes violently sick, for hours. I've never seen her like this. In utter anguish, we all feel that there's no way she's going to make it through what looks like a life-threatening episode. This is far worse than any of her previous chemo experiences. I am way beyond scared. Lord, what are we going to do? We're in Texas! Time seems to stand still as we pray desperately. Mom wants us to wait before calling 911, and shortly after we all pray, she miraculously begins to recover. Within the next few days she feels able to take the long Houston to Miami trip home. Thank you, Lord!

## Recovering

Statistics say people don't generally survive such advanced cancer, but my mother has now survived all of the chemo treatments. She's still in a weakened state, but I have hope that she's going to survive all of this. I don't want to think otherwise. Dad and I help her as much as we can, and draw closer to each other. Our church family and friends are a wonderful support system also.

Soon after her last chemo treatment, Mom's hair begins to grow back. Surprisingly, her formerly wavy hair starts coming in totally straight and auburn, the color she was born with (even though she'd gone totally gray many years before). She is thrilled to have her hair back and is amused by her new look. Later it returns to the way it was before, with a little help from a hair product. I'm glad she can find humor in little things like that.

As weeks turn into months, Mom has various physical struggles which creep in from time to time while her health is gradually improving. Then after five years, we celebrate that wonderful phrase, "cancer free!" But her energy level still isn't that good and she continues to have occasional symptoms that raise the question, "is it coming back?"

*Several years later my parents moved out of the Miami area and Dr. Johnson flew in one of his cancer patients and nurse in his private jet to visit Mom and hear her story. And of course, he was overjoyed to see Mom in a healthy state at that time. It's obvious that Dr. Johnson has great respect and admiration for my mother, through this loving and extraordinary visit.*

*Mom told me later that the visit was a good one and the patient was encouraged. Perhaps Mom's faith had more of a spiritual impact on her doctor than he let on. Was God's Divine intervention for him, and maybe the nurse — not just for the patient? Surely this highly unusual trip was the hand of God.*

# Mom's Calling and Legacy

It's just a few months after Mom's last dose of chemo. Our Associate Pastor has come to our house for a visit. "That's nice," I think, not realizing there's an additional purpose to this visit. He asks my parents if they would consider teaching the Young Adult Sunday School class. I'm shocked! Mom still isn't back to the energy level or emotional health that she had before the surgery. Dad would be there, but Mom would do all of the teaching. They agree to take some time to pray about it. Personally, I think the church has a nerve to even ask. Don't they know how sick she still is?

Against all logic, Mom and Dad agree to accept the job. I'm incredulous that they said yes. Doesn't Mom know what a drain this will be on her still weakened body, and the emotional energy she'll expend? I can tell she's hesitant and somewhat fearful, but she and Dad feel that God is in this. I guess I've kept God out of the equation, haven't I.

It doesn't take long for me to see how wrong I was. The young adults and my folks bond together as a close family. All their lives are enriched and inspired and Mom's health continues to improve. They have parties and a wonderful marriage enrichment retreat. When her cancer reoccurs, they storm Heaven in prayer, and bless her with phone calls, cards and visits. Later on, the class creates an album of memories for Mom and Dad to enjoy.

*I am almost overwhelmed by the fact that God changed Mom's fears into faith to teach the Sunday School class. The wonderful people there helped her as much as she helped them over the years, as I saw the power and grace of God at work. God, I think, likes to surprise us. I'm learning more and more about grace.*

In just about all of Mom's doctor visits, inpatient and outpatient hospital experiences, I have observed her telling the people about Jesus. Her testimony is very credible as they see how sick she is, yet she still maintains her trust in the Lord. Though prone to worry, Mom's faith never wavers. The more difficult her life becomes, the stronger her faith grows and is evident. Her Bibles are full of underlined verses and notes in the margins. I am aware of what was going on when she underlined some of them.

Mom puts her faith into writing also, as she has all of her life. Her poems are inspiring to everyone; she writes even while suffering, or because of it. Some of her poems have been published in our denomination's magazine through the years. She compiled a treasury of her poetry and prose for Dad, Judy and me - a memoir of her life's various seasons. I treasure it.

Now Mom has had another major setback. The cancer has come back and attached itself to the orb around her eye, the weakest part of her body (due to shingles over her eye years before). Surgery reduces the swelling but leaves her with two eyes that aren't level with each other. At first she wears an eye patch, but eventually her brain makes the adjustment so she can see a little better. Amidst all of this, she is creating three "roots" albums for Dad, Judy and me. Only Dad knows about the many hours she's working on this. I am totally surprised when she presents it to me!

*How I wish I'd expressed a greater degree of appreciation for this beautiful, sacrificial gift. I realize now how much love went into this wonderful book of family history, while she was struggling to see. I was always so caught up in my worries about her ups and downs that I had no emotional energy to really appreciate this work of art. I think that somehow she knows how much this means to me now.*

I believe that Mom has passed down to me her love for the arts. Some of her creations through the years were tabletop sand sculptures, junk art, short stories, poetry, playing the piano and accordion. She has always been an avid reader, devouring spiritual books. Listening to Christian music brings joy to her heart and I often hear her singing around the house.

One of her significant creations while in remission was a medical junk-art airplane she created and framed for Dr. Johnson. She presented this masterpiece to the doctor when he flew in his patient from Miami to meet Mom. Every one of the more than 13 items in this bi-plane work of art incorporates medical items ranging from pill bottle caps to tongue depressors. Cotton balls are the clouds. It is awesome! She took a picture of it, identifying each item on the back.

I love putting my own creative juices into pencil and crayon art in professional coloring books, play the piano a little (Dad taught me; he was our church organist) and love listening to music. I enjoy designing my own greeting cards, occasionally write poetry, and read continuously. Being creative is a joyful experience for me. I feel so happy when someone else is blessed by my efforts. Thank you, Mom, for being a creative influence on my life.

# Nearing the End

It's just over nine years since Mom's cancer first appeared, and now I'm suffering along with her as her last eight or nine months are a slow, downward spiral. I'm very thankful for the extra time we had with Mom and realize that she was spared those years for many reasons. God's timing is perfect, but I wonder, why didn't He heal her completely, to live a longer life? I don't know, but I am determined to trust Him, no matter what.

Mom's cancer has metastasized to her stomach and eventually requires a feeding tube. It's so painful for me to see her body wasting away. There's so much I'd like to be able to say to her, to comfort her, to express more love. I just can't get it out.

Several years ago, Mom told me she'd asked God that if she should have to suffer illness, that there would be no pain. All through her physical suffering, she has much discomfort, but never once has pain. She thanks the Lord for that.

The first of two very special requests Mom asked from God in her final months was to see Judy and her family. They live so far away, on the Pacific Coast. Mom's been eagerly awaiting the birth of Judy's daughter, Mom's first grandchild.

By the time Jenny is born, Mom's in pretty bad shape. When Judy's baby is cleared by the doctor to travel, Judy, Ken and Jenny fly in from Oregon. It's now early March 1986. Mom, though lying in a hospital bed and connected to tubes, is blessed to hold her precious almost-one-month-old granddaughter. It's a bittersweet, but God-ordained moment. I'm so glad this happened for all our sakes, but it is very hard to watch this hospital scene. There's no words to describe the emotional pain. I think I've numbed my mind a little, to get through it.

Dad gets to dote on his new grandchild, a respite from all the pain of seeing Mom suffer day after day. I'm an aunt for the first (and only) time, but my emotions are not enjoying it very much. Despite the pain, precious memories like these are treasures to keep forever.

# Thoughts of Heaven

Mom's death in mid–March 1986, at age 66, is very hard on all of us. She's too young to die! Mom and I were close in that I was very dependent on her, but we were not always very expressive of our deepest, intimate loving feelings. I feel some guilt for not being more verbally and physically caring during her nine years of cancer. She knew I loved her, though, and that I did the best I could.

As we plan the funeral, the thing I'm dreading the most is seeing her in the open casket at the viewing. I don't want to do this, but know I must for Dad's sake. God has to help me; I don't have the strength to look! When the time comes, the Lord gives me the most profound assurance that she is not there, but in Heaven, and will live on forever with Him. It's a revelation, a deep knowing, and a peace directly from God that sustains me during those hours of visitation. It also helps me let go, at least a little bit.

I increasingly realized that God knew just what I needed throughout Mom's final months and days. No detail escaped His attention. His grace was sufficient when I was weak.

He also reminded me, and continues to tell me, to live fully in the present, and to appreciate the people who love me and who mean the most to me.

I'm also made aware that this world is not our home. God's got an indescribably wonderful place prepared for us all. I believe I will see Mom again. Nothing can take away that hope.

***But I have digressed again:*** Back to 1980: I was holding on to hope for my own suddenly uncertain future which was starting to unravel again in a very frightening way for me.

# On My Own (But Not By Choice)

## God Interrupts My Plans, Again!

*"From one man He made every nation of men, that they should inhabit the whole earth; and He determined the times set for them, and the exact places where they should live."* (Acts 17:26.)

Summer 1980-October 1981
Miami and Fort Myers, Florida

Mom's cancer is in remission at this time and life is getting a bit easier for all of us. I've started to relax more and things are beginning to return to normal. After a delicious spaghetti supper (one of my favorites – did Mom plan this?) Mom says with a smile,

"Let's leave the dishes for a bit," and leads Dad and me into the living room. My curiosity is quickly replaced with a bombshell.

"Dad's going to retire from the Post Office in December and we've decided to move to Fort Myers as soon as we can sell the house and buy one there. You remember that we took a few trips there and really liked it."

Where did this come from? I haven't had a clue that they were even remotely thinking about leaving Hialeah. I feel a panic attack coming on.

"What am I going to do?" I ask her. "How can I leave my job after all these years?"

"Why do you think you have to move, too?" Mom asks. "It's not that far away, so we can visit each other often." Easy for her to say. She's sure matter-of-fact about this.

No, this is not acceptable to me. It's an almost three-hour drive between cities. I am over 30 but still afraid of being alone. Maybe I can transfer to the FAA in Ft. Myers, or some other agency. But I soon find out that there are no federal government positions available in Fort Myers. Now I feel like I'm beating my head against the wall. I don't see any solution to this problem and know that I'll have to stay here, at least temporarily, **by myself**.

I know I should have been on my own a long time ago, but being the dependent person I am, have put it off, always hoping the right guy would come along, marry me and we'd start a new life together. Things have changed in the early 80's, but there's still somewhat of a stigma about a single woman living alone. I use that as an excuse as I try to rationalize to myself why I'm almost 32 and still living with my parents. I wonder what I'm really afraid of.

In my still immature thinking, I feel hurt that Mom and Dad are moving without considering my own needs (looking back, I see how much growing up I had to do). So I fight it with my teeth clenched and a high degree of anxiety, but finally rent a nice little town home in Miami Lakes. It's in a pretty good neighborhood, in a cul-de-sac with only about nine or ten similar houses on the block. I feel pretty safe here. Since Mom and Dad haven't moved yet, they help me get set up.

This town home is very unique. It has a living/dining room on one side and a large bedroom on the other, connected by a long, narrow kitchen. There's a bathroom behind the dining room mirror and another behind the electric pullout bed; each side has large open-air closets. I'm amazed at this very practical layout, with a washer/dryer combo and a garbage compactor, along with all the usual kitchen appliances. I've never seen anything like it. It also has some furniture and is just perfect for my needs! Mom gives me a lot of kitchen supplies to start out with in my new life.

While being much better than living in an apartment, the expensive rent eats up one of my two monthly paychecks. For the first time in my career, I have to really count pennies. Any time I think I want to buy something extra, I have to ask myself if I really need it.

I adjust a little better than I thought I would, living by myself; in fact, I'm a little amazed. It's great to know I can do this! I don't feel too lonely, since my parents haven't moved yet, and they're close by. Living independently feeds my self-esteem. I believe the Lord was working in my mind when I didn't even know it, and kind of forced the issue when I needed to make some changes. He knew exactly when I'd be ready, even though I didn't.

Shortly before they move, Mom, Dad and I drive to Lakeland to visit Grandma and Grandpa Johnson. We attend church with them on Sunday, and during the service, the pastor asks anyone needing a job to stand for prayer. I feel somewhat frozen in time as I stand by my seat, and he prays over us! I sense right then that God is going to answer my prayer to find employment in Fort Myers. I don't think that specific prayer was a coincidence. I really don't want to stay in Miami with no family or close friends.

~

Mom and Dad move pretty quickly. I believe God intervened for them again. They sell their home at a great price and buy a nice home with the big kitchen that Mom had always wanted. The house is much larger than the one in Hialeah and in a nice neighborhood, convenient to everything. They are very happy!

I miss them so much, and now I'm so very lonely and miserable. I pray for God to open up a Government job for me, but despite frequent calls, nothing. Though I love my job here, I feel like it's my whole life. And that isn't enough. There are no singles my age at church and I have no real friends, the kind you spend leisure time with.

One morning I'm on my knees praying the same old prayer, and I ask God if He really cares about where I live. Right then, in faith, I finally completely surrender to God my desire to find a job in Fort Myers. Whatever He wants is what I want, no matter how I feel. It is an intense prayer time, and when I open my eyes, a brilliant stream of light angles over and covers me. I pick up my Bible and come across Acts 17:26.

I have learned that there is nothing as sweet as complete surrender to the Lord. But surrender does not come easily. Through the years I've struggled with it as more life-changing events developed and challenged my faith. This is called spiritual growth.

I feel sure God has a plan for me. And it seems like He is giving me a green light to seek a job in Fort Myers, even if it is not with the federal government.

# Transitions

Every weekend I travel to Fort Myers and pound the pavement seeking a job. It's so disappointing to find out that the pay scale in Fort Myers is drastically less than what I'm earning in Miami. I decide to sign up with an employment agency, but they don't give me much encouragement. It seems my lack of bookkeeping experience is keeping me from getting office management positions, and secretarial salaries are not nearly enough to sustain a single person. I only have one lead, which falls flat. But I'm determined to keep my options open. I try to get a job at a Christian school but the principal tells me that I'm overqualified and they can't pay me a salary remotely close to what I need. (Though I've always had a desire to work for a Christian organization, apparently God wants me in a secular business.)

Finally, I have an interview at a hospital management organization, which seems promising. My interview has gone well, although I wonder about some of the duties I'm told I'd be expected to perform. A yellow flag pops up in my mind, as I recall the land management organization that gave me the heebie jeebies. Someone else gets the job anyway, and years later I hear that this organization had some legal troubles and went out of business, just like that other one in Miami. Déjà vu!

These weekend trips are getting tiresome. I don't like to drive, especially on long trips, so sometimes I go Greyhound (many more hours). Once I took a friend with me, another time I hitched a ride with a family from work who were going to Fort Myers. It's great to be with my family, but I wonder how long I can keep this up.

∾

Finally, I have a good lead in my search for employment. A friend from the Fort Myers church works at a local law firm and has set up an interview for me. This turns out to be a different kind of interview. The head of the firm spends quite a bit of time with me, and though my portfolio is full of the accolades I think a boss would jump at, he doesn't seem to be impressed. He studies my paperwork some more, while I anxiously wait.

"Well, I'm not sure you really want to work here, or even that I want you. So here's what I'm going to do. I'm offering you a six-month trial period, and then we'll see where we go from there."

*"Oh, so I'm on trial,"* I think, *"at a law firm, no less. How ironic."* I'm glad he can't read my thoughts.

We haggle over my salary, which he tells me is classified information. I'm to tell no one how much I'm making, because it's more than some secretaries are earning after a few years at the firm. As it is, I'm taking a $110 a week pay cut, but I'm desperate. So I'm hired and begin working there in August 1981. *God knows what's in store for me there. If I knew, I would have soundly turned the job down.*

# Moving to Fort Myers

As I prepare to move from Miami, I have to break my lease. This means losing first and last months' rent and security deposit. My finances are not great; I could really use the money. My boss totally surprises me when he asks what the rent is, because he needs a place to live temporarily. He likes it as soon as he sees it and takes over my lease, later sending me the money I would have lost.

*What an unexpected blessing! I believe God's perfect timing and interventions are often connected to other events which He knows in advance.*

The Fort Myers church has a wonderful singles group, with lots of guys and gals around my age. I feel welcome immediately, and some of them come to Miami to help me move.

*I still have a mental image of the caravan of the U-Haul and vehicles going across Alligator Alley, the interstate that crosses the Everglades.*

I am overwhelmed by the eager willingness of everyone to help. God has blessed me with a new social life that is taking off once again.

## God's Project for Me at Fort Myers First Church

It isn't very long before I am approached by Frankie, a lady friend who was asked by some church members to consider establishing a library here. Would I like to help her? Wow, right up my alley. Frankie and I begin going through many dust-covered boxes of books in the church's storage room. I'm pretty excited about this project, and think it just might be Divine intervention, being the church didn't know of my previous library experience in Miami. Isn't it interesting how history repeats itself?

115

I'm excited at this new project and feel up to the task, even though I'm working full time now. So every weekend, Frankie and I organize and process the many books. It's a long and tedious job, doing everything by hand, but it's very rewarding to see the results. Sadly, Frankie passes away a short time later, and I'm suddenly the sole librarian at church.

Through the years, I'm known as "The Library Lady." It's more than a library to me; it's a place of grace, healing, practical Christian living, Bible study and education. Later on the library is moved from a small room in a back corner of the church to a bigger room across from the sanctuary. More people come in now, as the library becomes more visible.

# My New Home

After living a few months with Mom and Dad, I realize I need my own place. Elaine, a realtor from church, helps me find something affordable. I am so excited to buy a nice furnished singlewide mobile home in North Fort Myers. This is one of the few mobile home parks where you own your own lot, also. It's just the right size for my needs and has a large porch addition, so I can have our singles group come over occasionally. The drive to work is short and convenient, and church and the shopping mall are just a little further.

Because I left the federal government service after 15 years, I was able to take out my retirement money. That, plus my savings while living with my parents gives me enough to buy my new home with cash (and a small loan from Mom and Dad.) I never dreamed I'd be able to own something so soon! I believe God used my break in government service to enable me to afford a home.

This mobile home park is nicer than most in my price range. Most of the residents are retired, so the streets are quiet and I feel safe. You often see people riding 3-wheeler bikes around the park grounds. I also have good next-door neighbors who are very friendly and watch over me.

I am ecstatic to own my very own home! I am so thankful!

But life takes on another curve, as some unexpected experiences loom ahead, yet prove once again that nothing takes God by surprise. He will work all things for my good. It will help to remember that.

# Home At Last (But Not At Once)

## Sometimes Plan A Comes After Plan B

*"My times are in your hands."* (Psalm 31:15a.)

1981-1982

Fort Myers, Florida

### The Firm

I thought I was hired as a legal secretary. Well, that's not the plan right now, apparently. I'm assigned to the office manager and on my very first day, am put on the switchboard because the receptionist is on vacation. Instant panic sets in. I've never worked a switchboard in my 16 years of secretarial work! After maybe five minutes of instruction, I'm now on my own. The phone on the 9-line switchboard rarely stops ringing, giving me mere seconds to look up the many extensions. At the same time, people are coming up to the window for help. I am way beyond stressed! What have I gotten myself into?

After lunch, the boss has mercy and assigns a secretary to the switchboard. My duties are split between the office manager and the collections department. Even here, I get minimal instructions. I don't even know what questions to ask.

On my second day, I am reprimanded somewhat harshly for tearing a check incorrectly when I made a typing mistake (who types checks, anyway?). That puts my already teetering stress level over the edge. Trying to keep my emotions in check is a real battle. When I arrive at Mom and Dad's house after this gruelingly long day, I burst into the room and fall into Mom's arms, sobbing my heart out. This <u>never</u> happens! I'm a grown woman, but I want my mommy. I'm at my wits' end, and I've just started this job. I pray fervently for God's grace.

Everyone but me goes to lunch at noon, while I work the switchboard. My lunch is from 1 – 2 p.m. I also man the switchboard the first and last half-hour of each day. That's easier on me, because very few people call or come to the office then. Occasionally, though, I'm put in difficult situations with aggressive people at the lobby window or on the phone. I feel very intimidated and want to run away or bury myself in a hole. But I guess God won't let me.

My job assignments still aren't very clear to me, and I struggle to find any kind of rhythm in my working habits. I knew, coming in, that this would be different from my FAA workplace, but this radical change is mind-blowing.

I am happy to share an office with two other secretaries about my age, who are very nice to me. We talk a little, but too much conversation is frowned upon. Upper management sometimes comes to check on us; production is key. We are typing non-stop with two ten-minute breaks and an hour lunch. At least I have two friends here.

I could almost cry at how I'm looked upon as being a 'nobody.' I feel invisible. Few of the attorneys know my name, even after several months. A smile or hello to me is a rare occurrence from most of the staff. Adding insult to injury, I routinely have to empty ash trays in the lobby at the end of the day. This is humiliating to me, especially after all the royal treatment I had in my Miami job.

"Lord, why did you put me into this degrading atmosphere?" I pray. "You know I need this job. Flood me with Your grace and strength. I can't make it without You." If I didn't need the money, I'd be leaving faster than the roadrunner, beep-beeping anyone in my way.

Every morning I pray as I leave for work, and the Lord does sustain me through all this misery. At least I get lots of fresh air and exercise at lunchtime, as I walk around town or shop after I grab a quick sandwich. Looking back, I guess that was part of God's plan to keep me sane and healthy.

# Day of Reckoning

It's about two months before my six-month trial period ends and I'm just randomly thinking, meditating and praying about the job one Saturday at home. Suddenly a voice in my mind says that I'm going to be moved out of this job, with a specific date in February. This is not my own wishful thinking; I feel like it is God speaking. This brings me some peace and hope. After awhile, though, the thought leaves my mind and I wonder if I imagined it.

It's a late afternoon in February when the head attorney calls me into his office. He reminds me of our six-month trial period agreement and basically tells me that it's not working out.

"I have no problem with your work, but you just don't fit in with 'the family.' Everyone likes you, though"

*O-kaayy.., what's he saying here? Is he actually firing me? That never entered my mind as a possibility. I have noticed that just about everyone, including secretaries, constantly works overtime. I never do, but then again, they never ask. They all participate in company social events in their free time, too. Maybe that's why I don't fit in with the firm's agenda, or maybe I'm just not assertive or ambitious enough.*

As he's been talking, I've observed him holding five checks which he's apparently intentionally placed in his hand like a fan. He then says with a smile that doesn't quite reach his eyes,

"I know you like working here (*are you kidding??!*), but I have to let you go."

I'm thinking (and about to say) "Whatever gave you *that* idea? Boy, if you only knew how I *really* feel about this workplace" – but I do see those checks! So I bite my tongue and happily take the money I feel I've more than earned.

He tells me I can go home now (it's after 4 p.m.) but I decide to finish my day like a normal one, working my last half-hour at the switchboard. Near the end of that shift, one of the upper-level secretaries leaves me with an "in the future, do it this way" parting shot. She doesn't know what's just happened. I nod and act, to her and the rest of the crew when I leave, as though nothing unusual has occurred.

God's amazing grace enables me to leave there with my head held high, believing He's got a better plan. By the time I get to my car, the shock has worn off and I smile and thank God for getting me out of that horrible job. Instead of tearing out of there like a NASCAR driver, I'm calm and relieved. I remember that voice in my head from two months ago; the date was almost exactly what I heard. It had to be God. Yes!

*I believe He put me in this job temporarily to teach me humility as I emptied ash trays and was nameless to most of their workforce. In my past posh positions and many performance awards, I could see some egotistical professional pride creeping in, which I think God didn't like. Though I still have self-esteem issues in other areas, perhaps I had been unconsciously flaunting my efficiency to impress people.*

*I also believe that I needed to know how the private sector works. It opened my eyes to the safe cocoon that government service was for me; and how different a public service job is compared to the production quotas and pressure of making money for the companies of private industry. Though I've always been a diligent, hard worker, you might say I caught a glimpse of 'the real world.'*

# The Next Steps

Five weeks' pay sustains me quite well, another blessing from the Lord. I have some fun with friends, as I continue to check the few government agencies in the area. One day it pays off. The U.S. Geological Survey needs a secretary and the hiring freeze is about to be lifted. I complete the paperwork, and have some more leisure time while I wait on the usual red tape. It's a part-time GS-4, compared to my Miami full-time GS-6, but still a lot more money than I made at the Firm. I am very grateful.

My mind and emotions are settling down now. I'm so glad to be getting back into government employment and its great benefits. But the phone call I just got has stirred up the waters – again! It's the Fort Myers FAA Tower Chief!

"My secretary has unexpectedly had to move out of state. Are you still interested in the position?" (ya' think?)

This is a full-time GS-5 (much better!) and would bring me back to my FAA career. Here I am again, mind spinning with jumbled thoughts. I really want this FAA job, but I've committed to this other one. What do I do? First no government job; now I have two! I blurt out,

"Oh my, yes! But I just accepted a position with the Geological Survey and am waiting to be picked up. The paperwork is already being processed." I'm excited and upset at the same time.

"Well, we're still in a hiring freeze and don't know if and when it will be lifted. Why don't you report to work when they're ready for you. Should our freeze be lifted, you can do a resignation-transfer."

*Wow, I didn't know I could do that. Good solution!*

~

After being unemployed for less than six weeks, I've now begun working for the Geological Survey. The atmosphere is a stark contrast from the Miami FAA environment. It's a small office in the old federal building downtown. There are radiators in the hallways, which is really strange for Southwest Florida. The inside walls are dull and dingy in the musty-smelling hallways. Homeless people sometimes sleep on the steps of the building. The furniture and office equipment look pretty old, though I do feel like I've come back home to some familiar government office surroundings.

Most of the workforce spend the day in the field testing well water, so it's literally earthy and very casual. I'm used to suits and dress-up; the men are sometimes shirtless. The people are very nice and likeable, though, and treat me, the only female, with respect and dignity. The office has no filing system, so I organize all of their many drawers of files. I learn a little about water management in the process. Now I know what aquifers are. I'm also happy to have a friend who works in my building on another floor. We occasionally get together for lunch and outside of work.

Once my project is finished, I run out of work, and become bored. I'm glad to get back into the federal working environment, though, and to have money again while I'm hopefully waiting to get back with the FAA.

I stop to count my blessings. Escaping from the law firm into this very laid-back office is like comparing my move from New York to Florida. What a contrast! This in-between job shortens my break in government service, which will prove to be very significant years down the road.

I've got an idea; I'll call my friends from the law firm to get together for lunch. Their office isn't far from here. I'm feeling a little diabolical. As we catch up on things, I casually tell them about my new job's salary and benefits. Their jaws drop as I speak. I think my salary is *far* higher than theirs, even after their five years at the firm. They are sincerely happy for me, though. My leaving the firm was never discussed in that place of secrets, so they didn't know the reason for my sudden absence. I feel like I've been vindicated. It does give me a feeling of great satisfaction!

# Finally "Home Where I Belong"

## May 1982

As the Tower Chief predicted, my resignation-transfer occurs, within just ten weeks. It's like I've come back home – now to the FAA's Southwest Florida International Tower (RSW)! I'm again working in the Air Traffic Division. God has brought all this to pass, full circle, and I am so thankful!

I'm surprised to see how much smaller this facility is than the huge Miami ARTCC where I'd worked for 15 years. There are only a few radar scopes here. Miami had a large room full of many rows of them, because it's an en route radar center. Miami Center was located several miles apart from Miami Tower and Miami International Airport. This Fort Myers facility functions as Approach Control as well as the Tower operation, so it's a completely different environment.

It's pretty exciting to me that I'm hired in the midst of this brand new airport relocating from Page Field. Fort Myers is in the midst of a population explosion and has outgrown the old airport, which will later be used exclusively for general aviation aircraft.

I'm so excited to watch the pre-assembled tower put in place as our part of the airport is nearing completion. All the offices are on the ground floor, but I enjoy going to the tower cab to take in the beautiful view. It won't be long now before the airport is officially open.

This airport is beautiful! Driving in to work each morning, I see lots of Florida wading birds around the lake on the airport property. One morning I saw a pair of sandhill cranes doing a graceful mating dance. I have been thrilled to see their new babies born and growing up as I drive in to work. From the tower cab, I once saw a family of otters crossing the taxiway. Wild hogs and giant fox squirrels are some of the unexpected sightings I've enjoyed occasionally. The Port Authority stays busy keeping the runway clear. They often use Jet, the dog, to chase off wildlife. On rare occasions, an alligator might have to be removed from the runway.

I believe the Lord worked through circumstances at just the right time: I re-entered the federal workforce just months before the Civil Service Retirement System drastically changed. I had a choice to go into the new system, or remain in the old. The old one was very definitely better! God's timing gave me a lasting financial benefit.

# Across the Years at RSW Tower

I'm a little disappointed that I have to share an office with the Airway Facilities secretary. Our desks are adjoining so I don't have much privacy. She's nice and we get along fine, but I miss having my own private office. After several years the offices are moved around and I have my own space. Then years later a new wing is added to the building, providing me with the largest office I've ever had, complete with upgraded equipment and furniture. I'm back to feeling classy and important, but in a more casual atmosphere than Miami. The people here are very down-to-earth and pretty relaxed, though I can see on the controllers' faces when the air traffic is extra busy or challenging.

I was pretty happy working at Miami ARTCC, but working here is much more suited to my personality. Here I can be 'the real me' and am not pressured into doing anything I don't want to do in my free time. No one here tries to make me into someone I'm not.

Technology changes my job drastically. Computers entered into our world shortly after I arrived at RSW, and I have had to learn various programs as they were added. Before I retire (years down the road), I compile a procedures manual, and also train the supervisors in Time and Attendance reporting procedures which have changed many times over the years.

My duties have evolved into Administrative Assistant, Office Automation and Office Manager, so I am thrilled when the FAA reclassifies my job just a few years before I retire. I'm promoted to GS-7, a significant pay increase. Yippee! I never thought I'd see *that* day!

I've had three good managers to work for during my 20 years at the Tower. I've been very blessed by working here, for many reasons. I truly believe God put me here.

*Over the years I was able to pay back the retirement money I'd withdrawn when I left Miami, so when I retired at age 55, I received a very good retirement based on my 'high 3' salary. This too was significant and God's timing.*

# Another Divine Intervention – For Someone Else

I'm still working at the time, about two or three years from retiring. The Airway Facilities secretary recently retired, and no bids have been received for the position. Desperate for a secretary, the powers that be are considering waiving the requirement for a present or past federal employee to fill the job. When the Manager asks if I know of anyone needing a job. I eventually think to call the church. I find out that Linda, our pastor's wife, is looking for work and has secretarial experience in private industry. Because of the pressing need, they receive that hiring exception.

Linda is now working for A.F., right across the hall from my office. We get to chit chat sometimes, and I help her adjust to government employment.

*Linda has thanked me many times for connecting her to this position. She loves her job and her career advanced through the years, also. I feel privileged to be part of God's plan for her.*

# My Controller Friends at the Tower

Over the years, I've come to enjoy and connect with the air traffic controllers. I know they like me, but don't realize how much until years later, on that one day I will never forget.

*I'm in the Break Room, and one of the controllers has an odd expression on her face. I wonder what's going on, as other controllers come in and sit down, looking at me. In the next moment, I am presented with a pretty plant and a "thank you" greeting card. I thank them, but notice they can't wait for me to open the card, which is bulging through the envelope. When I see the contents, I am about to fall over, and seem to have lost my voice (and mind).*

### It's a large <u>stack</u> of one hundred dollar bills!

*After I can breathe again I ask,*

*"What is this for?"*

*One of the controllers beams, and says,*

*"This is just to show our personal appreciation for all you do for us. Everyone, including supervisors and staff, participated and signed the card."*

*They really do love me. I thank each one personally as they come in for their different shifts. What a blessing that lives forever in my cherished memories.*

Though I've enjoyed all these years working as a secretary/office manager, after 35 years I am *so* ready to retire. I've had a hand-made calendar of 'months before retirement' on my refrigerator for two years. The day I turn 55, I decide, is my last day of work.

On that day, some of the controllers who can be spared from duty, along with supervisors, RSW staff and my pastor attend a retirement luncheon in my honor. Their cards, personal gifts, heartfelt remarks and wishes touch me just as much as the Great Gift. I tell them through my somewhat shaky emotions that I was made richer by knowing them, literally!

This has been a birthday I'll never forget! I'm officially retired!!

*The Government has been good to me, and its financial benefits extend into my retirement. I don't take that for granted.*

But I've digressed again.

Back to the 1980's:

*God has shown me much favor in my career, but I'm asking Him, when will He show me favor in finding a good man?*

# Men in My Life

## God Gets Involved in My Choices

*"In his heart, a man plans his course, but the Lord determines his steps."* (Proverbs 16:9)

Late 1970's-1980
Miami

My dream since childhood was to marry a "handsome prince" when I turned 20 or so, raise a family, and hopefully be a stay-at-home mom. I'm a romantic by nature, and sometimes live in a fairy-tale world. Yes, I played with Barbie dolls and created paper doll designer dresses; I did all the girlie things. Yet I've never bonded with babies; in fact, they kind of scare me. I have no idea why.

I must be a late bloomer, because I am 19 when I have my first real date. It's at a church function in Miami, and I only accept the date because no one else asks me. He's nice enough, I have a good time, but he's definitely not for me.

My thoughts keep returning to those last moments with my youth leader friend from New York. I can't seem to let go of the possibility of continuing our relationship, to see where it might lead. Is this my own romantic nature on overload, or is God leading me?

135

I'll never know if I don't take some action, so I've decided to write a letter to him. Lo and behold, he's written back!

I'm really enjoying his letters, which give me the courage to invite him down for a visit. I didn't expect such a quick response, but he's taken me up on my offer. I'm really excited and nervous at the same time as that day arrives. He's staying in my sister's bedroom at my parents' house and I'm sharing my room with Judy. Close quarters for sure, as she's been teasing and razzing me a lot, of course. I try to ignore her and decide to just enjoy myself.

He and I have fun sightseeing the tourist attractions in the general vicinity. Although we get along well, and certainly aren't bored, I don't think either of us is seeing a future together. Yeah, there's a little bit of romance, but something's not there, you know? We both avoid talking about 'us' and just when I'm at the point of wondering what happens next, he abruptly packs up and leaves. I'm kind of stunned, but relieved in a way.

A week later, I go to the mailbox and find a letter from him. I anxiously tear open the envelope. He's apologized for his abruptness, honestly describing his confused feelings. So I guess it wasn't God who initiated this plan of mine. I can't say I regretted it, though. Some fun along with lessons learned isn't a bad place to be.

Through the years, Mom and I talk, laugh, cry and sometimes giggle over my romantic prospects, or lack thereof. She gives me pointers on attracting guys and dating. She's a romantic at heart too, but also tries to keep me balanced in my thinking. Dad doesn't usually say much, but if I date someone with a beard or hair longer than his collar, Dad wonders humorously what I see in him. At my age, I can't be too choosy and have to look beyond the external appearance to the heart of the person, which is what we all should do anyway. As each birthday passes, I feel more and more lonely, praying for a good man to show up in my life.

I date a few men I know at work, but it's often my strict upbringing and religious beliefs which seem to get in the way. The occasional dates with some guys from church seem to go nowhere. Then there are the two younger friends-only guys Dianne and I hung out with years ago. They're still single, but it seems like I'm not what they are looking for; I wonder why not, since by now, the age difference shouldn't matter. Well, the fact that they're each dating someone at the moment could be a factor.

## An Act of Desperation?

August 1977, the big 3-0. I am not happy at this age milestone, depressed at the thought of being an 'old maid.' Will I ever find someone to love and be loved by? Suddenly, out of the blue, a friend of Mom's from church approaches me with a gleam in her eye. She has a brother my age who's recovering from a divorce and she thinks we could be good for each other. He has a young son whom he's raising, and she says that he is a wonderful Christian man. The only problem – he lives in North Carolina! At her suggestion I write him a letter and he writes back, with a picture of himself and his son. Wow, is he ever good looking; I'm almost drooling.

After a few months of mutually friendly letters, I invite him to come down for a visit (déjà vu?) Will this long-distance relationship bode better than my other one? His letter kind of indicates he's not really ready to take that step. I guess he's still hurting and afraid of any kind of relationship. Somehow, though, between our letters and his sister's encouragement (or pushiness) he invites me up there.

## An Interesting Amtrak Encounter

Since I don't want to fly or drive, I take Amtrak again. This is a little shorter ride than the New York one; it's about 18 hours. I'm surprised and maybe a little startled when a good-looking man, probably around my age, confidently takes the seat beside me, as he casually asks if I mind that he does. I don't know what to think of him yet and try to bury myself in my book. He wants to be friendly, though, and strikes up a pleasant enough conversation. I tell him about my upcoming visit and show him the picture of the 'pen pal' I'm traveling to meet.

He seems a bit of a flirt (*someone across the aisle asks me if I need help! Remember my Miami bus ride?*). I've got it under control, though, and he seems pretty safe – especially when he tells me he's engaged and meeting up with his fiancé at his stop in North Carolina. "*Oh, so we're going to be together for the duration of my trip.*" I think. "*Wonder what will happen next?*"

It doesn't take very long for me to see that this handsome 'charmer' is *pretty* friendly for someone planning to get married! Thankfully, He doesn't try anything I'd call improper. But he wants me to go with him to the lounge car for a drink. Turning him down only slightly discourages him. But then again, I'm not sure how much I want to.

This trip is overnight, and I've brought a blanket. It's virtually impossible for me to sleep in Amtrak's reclining seat with this interesting man beside me. I feign abruptly turning over in my sleep, tugging my blanket tightly over me when he tries to pull a corner of it over himself. Guess I had him fooled, he confesses in the morning that he tried to share my blanket. He buys me breakfast, and I have to admit he's a pretty decent guy as he tells me more about himself.

He certainly has kept the ride from being boring! Needless to say, I haven't gotten past the first few pages of my book.

## Another Bubble Burst

As I disembark from the train, I am thrilled to finally meet the man I have known only through letters. As we get to know each other during the 45-minute ride to his home, I can already tell that he is a man with many good qualities. I stay with his parents, who are wonderful, godly people and I'm happy they like me so much. I can see that I have an ally with his Mom especially.

He doesn't take off work, so I spend more time with his folks than with him. We do spend the evenings and weekend doing things together, though nothing I'd call romantic. (I had more romance on Amtrak then here.) I really like him a lot, but can see that he's nowhere near ready.

I have enjoyed my time there very much, but when he takes me to the Amtrak station, saying goodbye is awkward and kind of abrupt like it was with my youth leader friend. I write to him later, trying to encourage him but also curious to know why he showed so little interest in me. He writes back a very kind and nice letter, being honest about himself and assuring me that the problem wasn't me. How strange when history repeats itself!

I have found out that trying to make something happen doesn't usually work, especially if it's ahead of God's timing. Usually, if God's not in it, the doors will close, or a red flag will pop up. Lesson learned.

*I also found out that years later he met a wonderful woman, when he was ready for another relationship. He eventually married her. Perhaps I was instrumental in part of his healing; if so, I'm really happy about that.*

# 1981-1983

## Fort Myers

I'm grateful that my Fort Myers church has such a nice singles group, with both gals and guys my age. We all enjoy being with each other, and eventually I have a few dates, but they are more friendships than the kind of relationships with a future. It's great to have all these friends; this takes the sting out of my extended times of dateless-ness.

## Broken Hearts

Finally, I have met a Christian man with whom I seem to 'click.' We have quite a bit in common, have lots of fun, go to church and Bible studies together, and he has quite an effect on me. After about six months of dating, we are engaged. I think I love him, and have told him that I do. I feel sure that he loves me. But he senses that something isn't right on my end and tells me so. I don't want to admit to myself that I have pushed aside a few recurring issues which have bothered me. I guess you could call them yellow flags that I've tended to ignore.

He's getting a house ready for us and when I'm over there helping him paint, I see my 8X10 picture on his dresser. My internal reaction surprises me upon seeing it. My mind senses a strange feeling of stark reality; wow he really does love me. I matter a lot to this man. It's a very strange feeling. Have I been living a pretend life in this very real relationship? Attributing this to pre-wedding jitters, I again push the thought aside and go ahead a few days later to shop for my wedding gown and bridesmaid dress. The gown I select is elegant in its simplicity, but not what I'd pictured myself wearing, in my younger, dreamy days. (Could this be my subconscious mind at work?)

I have way too many confusing thoughts which are growing as the wedding date is approaching, and everything is suddenly very real. One day something that is significant to me happens, and from deep within my spirit I realize that this marriage may not be God's plan for me, or for him either. I think I've just been wanting to avoid facing this head-on.

Mom asks me some pertinent questions which give me some insight and counsel. Right then, I know that I have to make a clear-cut decision, immediately! It's a tough choice to make, because my heart and emotions are so involved, and I still feel torn – and in panic mode.

"God, please guide me," I plead. Some specific scriptures come to me, prompted by the Lord, and I decide to write my thoughts down. As I write, I already know my answer. I make the final decision to break it off.

Now I have to break the news to him. This is excruciatingly difficult for me as I face this daunting task. Our differences aren't glaringly obvious and it's hard for me to explain to him. But God gives me assurance and peace that I am doing the right thing. I believe He is the One intervening in the first place.

My fiancé's reaction is understandable, which makes me feel terrible. My emotions are on a never-ending roller-coaster ride. I feel so bad for the hurt I've caused him and his family. But marrying out of God's plan would bring greater pain, and that thought brings me a measure of relief. The Lord helps me through the guilt. I feel awkward at church for a while, but life goes on, and soon I again involve myself in our singles group.

*As I consider God's part in this now broken relationship, I come to believe that He waved a red flag after I didn't respond* to His yellow ones in my heart and mind. With a feeling devoid of peace, He got my attention just in time. I guess it took some time because my emotions got in the way of hearing Him clearly. I can see now that lack of peace or uneasy feelings are interventions in my mind from the Lord.

My experience also makes me realize that Christian mothers are God's special gifts to their children. Mine was not perfect, but had much insight and understanding into who I was as I was growing up, and what I needed. I thank God for the lessons she taught me, her guidance through the years and especially during my decision to break my engagement. I believe God used her wisdom to intervene in my thought processes when I was on the wrong track.

# Another New Start

I have already sold my furnished mobile home (pre-broken engagement) to of all people, my next-door neighbors! They decided to buy it as an investment. I believe this was Divine intervention. I got a good price and everything was completed in a relatively short time. So I've been living with Mom and Dad until I can find something else. I wonder if I can afford a real house. A mobile home is adequate, but it sure would be nice to own an actual house.

I'm pretty excited now, going house-hunting with my realtor from church. I'm discouraged by the prices of the homes she shows me. I can't afford those mortgage payments. But then we come across an older, smaller two-bedroom home which just might be made for me. It has a large 'Florida room', a screened-in porch and a pretty yard with fruit trees. The lemon tree is huge; guess I'll be making lemonade and lemon meringue pies.

If they accept my offer, I'll be able to swing it. They counter with one I can live with, so it's a done deal. I can hardly believe I own a house! When I excitedly receive the keys at the closing, the title insurance agent says, "That is one happy young lady!" God is so good!

Now I'm having a ball buying furniture for my entire house with the proceeds from my mobile home sale. The location is great! It is only a few blocks from Mom and Dad, closer to work and church, and close to shopping. What more could I ask for?

## Company's Coming

I've settled in now, and am starting to feel a little lonely living by myself, even though Mom and Dad are close by. My phone rings. It's Mom.

"There's a cat standing at our back door, asking for a home. Want to come see?"

She's a cute black and white young cat, and I know I want her. I take her home with me and she lives in my porch. She lets me pet her, pick her up occasionally and snuggle. I name her Huggie. She's not a lap cat and doesn't have Tiger's personality, but is company. I'm happy to have her.

I'm grateful to have very good next-door neighbors. After living there almost a year, I find out they've been paying for my garbage pickup! I'd thought it was included in the property taxes. All the neighbors closest to my house are friendly and look out for me.

As Thanksgiving approaches, I think God wants me to share my blessings with my neighbors. So I invite some of them over to share Thanksgiving with my parents and me in my new home. It's a nice time for everyone and another memory which brings warmth to my heart.

I believe God helped me find a house of my own, located close to Mom and Dad. Mom was still in remission, but the cancer would return. It was again God's timing for me to be close by.

God continued to guide me though His Word, and through the Holy Spirit. He was certainly growing my faith. Why did I still think everything was all up to me?

*I decided to stop trying so hard to find a man and just enjoy life.*

# The Love of My Life

## Divine Intervention of the Best Kind

*"And now these three remain: faith, hope and love.*
*But the greatest of these is love."* (I Corinthians 13:13)

### May 1985

Mona, our Singles leader is such a matchmaker! Her goal is to get everyone in the Singles Group married off. She thinks she's subtle about it, and it's comical at times, but always grounded in prayer. She and her husband Charles love each one of us dearly. I'm thankful for them and can use all the help I can get.

I've noticed a good-looking man who started attending our services recently. He sits toward the back and never hangs around long enough to meet (not that I'd introduce myself, anyway). I'm curious though, and find myself looking for him each time I'm at church. I haven't asked Mona about him yet (not knowing that Mona planted herself between him and the door last Sunday, to briefly interrogate him as only she can do).

Now, a week later, Mona glides slyly over to me and gives me the little scoop she's been able to find out. His name is Dan, he's 47 (but certainly doesn't look it), seems nice – and she personally invited him to our Sunday School class. She can be persuasive at times, so I wonder if he'll show up.

My heart starts to accelerate when he enters our Sunday School room the following Sunday. I'm super-conscious of him during the lesson, and after we dismiss I get up my nerve and actually speak to him. I find out that Dan works for Ford as a Parts Salesman. After just a brief conversation, he asks me out! Wow, you never know about these quiet types! I give him my phone number and we sit together in church. I'm trying not to act as giddy as I feel.

As I anticipate our upcoming dinner date, I feel like an excited teenager. I change my outfit a few times, wanting to look my best. I wonder what he's really like, and hope he likes me. Our first date is very nice, at an upscale restaurant on Fort Myers Beach. It goes quite well, with no awkwardness that some first dates usually have.

My first impression of Dan is that he is a calm, dignified man, who carries himself gracefully, with class. He has kind eyes and seems genuine and down to earth. I can tell that he's a hard worker and since he has a long career with Ford, I figure he's dependable. I'm blown away when he tells me he has five grown children. This man is continuing to amaze me.

I'm surprised at how comfortable I feel, and know I want to see him again. I guess he feels the same way, because I've just gotten home from our second date. I really enjoy being with him and glad to find that we have similar tastes and interests – a good sign! At the end of our date, he tells me he's flying to Indiana to visit family for a week. I guess life for me will quiet down for a while.

∾

Dan has made quite an impression on me. I'm missing him already, and it's only been a few days since he left. A knock on my door interrupts my daydreaming. I open it to find a gorgeous bouquet of flowers with a "thinking of you" card on it from him. I'm pretty overwhelmed. "This guy is a keeper" I think. He calls me a few days later. He'll be back very soon, and we'll pick up where we left off! Wow, this could really turn out to be something; could he be "the one?" Too soon to be thinking those thoughts; but I can't help it.

We get to know each other better and spend more and more time together. Soon he wants to introduce me to his two beautiful daughters and their boyfriends. I'm really nervous about meeting them, and think things are moving kind of fast. I'm relieved when both his daughters welcome me warmly and seem happy for him. Later on I'll meet his three sons – one lives locally and two in Indiana.

Dan is a good, decent Christian man, and there's just something about him that seems a lot different and better for me than any of my previous relationships. We've been dating regularly, and though I can't actually define the exact moment I realized that I "fell in love," I know he has been in my thoughts constantly. The people at work tell me that my face lights up at the mention of his name. Sometimes they tease me about having my head in the clouds. We are engaged after only three months. This time I am sure. We're going to get married in December, just seven months from the day we first met. I can hardly believe this is happening! And a Christmastime wedding is so romantic!

Dan has won over my Mom's heart, too, in the gentle way he relates with her as cancer begins to return to her body. Dan's sister has cancer also, so we share in the pain of the struggle of cancer, but find comfort in the hope of heaven. It's ironic that my mom and Dan's sister are both named Irene, and they are battling late-stage cancer at the same time. But knowing Christ, both have peace, the meaning of their name. This painful but spiritual connection Dan and I have brings us even closer to each other.

Mom and Dad both say that Dan's the kind of man they always wanted me to marry, even before he asks. Mom tells me later that Dad said he's glad Dan works in the auto industry, since I've had so many car problems. Dad really likes Dan, too. "Now that's what I'm talking about" he says, or something like it

# The Wedding

## December 7, 1985

I'm so excited, planning our wedding! The first thing I do is shop for a wedding gown. I'm really disappointed that Mom is too sick to go with me, but as I try on gowns, the sadness over Mom turns to joy in what I'm now doing. I've found the perfect gown, at a terrific price. It's gorgeous, traditional white and lacy, decorated with some pearls and it has a long train. I feel like the princess I imagined way back in my childhood dreams!

The bridesmaid dresses I've selected are teal and light green, to blend in with the greens of the Christmas season. On one of Mom's 'good days' she was able to shop for a beautiful dress; she looks very much 'mother of the bride.' My large bouquet will be white carnations, mums and red roses. The guys will be in black tuxedos. I am so excited!

My church friends are really helpful in planning the reception and other odds and ends. A church family friend decorates the church with a large arrangement of red poinsettias, huge Christmas wreaths on the walls and red velvet bows on alternate pews. My closest friends gave me a bridal shower, with lots of lacy things to take on our honeymoon, if you get my drift.

I wake up immersed in joy and excitement as the big day has finally arrived! My friend from the Geological Survey, who is my Maid of Honor, is staying with me and she does my nails and helps me get ready at home. My sister, who's in her seventh month of pregnancy can't fly out from Oregon, but calls with heartfelt wishes. I am so blessed! Is this really happening? I can hardly believe it, a dream coming true.

When I arrive at the church, I can see that everything is under control. I see Dan is already there and I quickly hide so he doesn't see me before the ceremony. Dan's daughters, who are my bridesmaids, come in with me as we all do the final touches on our hair, etc. Okay, I'm ready!

I will never forget walking down the aisle on Dad's arm, with countless thoughts falling over each other, and seeing my sweet husband-in-a-few minutes looking very handsome, totally focused on me. As I approach the front of the church, I am so blessed to see Mom in the front row, looking really beautiful, even though her body is now becoming ravaged with cancer. Looking at her at this special moment, I realize that you really can't see how very sick she is. It has to be God's grace. I am so very grateful that she can share in this wonderful time of my life.

*This, you know, was the other request Mom asked of the Lord in her final months – to see me married. He answered her prayer!*

Time seems suspended in these brief but sacred moments. My nerves and emotions are giving me fits, but when I take Dan's hand I calm down in just a few minutes.

Our ceremony, performed by Pastor Mike Ross, is very spiritual, as we begin our marriage with Christ at the center. The music, atmosphere and the pastor's words and scriptures are so special to me. I can hardly believe it, we're man and wife now; I'm Mrs. Dan Deniston!

∼

I'm not very aware of who's actually there until we stand in the receiving line. A van from Miami brought some of our church family friends. My friend Kathy, the secretary from the FAA in Miami (who I worked with the longest) is here. Several of my Ft. Myers FAA friends have come, and others sent gifts. The reception is fun, and I get to visit a little with everyone. Wow, the gift table is full! We have lots of gifts and cash. My boss from Miami sent us a wedding gift with regrets at not being able to come. I'd told him one reason I was moving was to find a Christian man to marry; and that's exactly what happened!

Dan has hidden his car in the hospital parking lot not far from the church, so it doesn't get 'decorated' like so many in the past have done. A friend from my FAA office has hired a limo to take us from the church to our car. How funny; we had everyone fooled! What a blast!

It's such a surreal feeling that we're married now, as we drive off to begin our honeymoon and our new life! We spend a fun and wonderful week in various cities in Florida, then return to a hard reality when we get back home. Mom is in the hospital, in serious condition. I'm so thankful for Dan to be there for me, and to go with me to the hospital all those nights.

I believe it was God who brought Dan and me together in the denomination we both grew up in. It's not a coincidence that Dan 'felt' it was time for a change of churches when he started attending mine. I never would have met him, if he hadn't followed his heart. So I see that it wasn't me who set this up; God did. And I think it didn't happen until I let go and let God bring about our meeting each other.

God sure intervened in His timing: I met Dan as Mom's cancer was coming back. He was my stronghold during those many hard days and nights. Mom died three months after we got married.

# A House and a Home

Dan and I live in my house for two years and then look for a larger and newer one. We house-hunt with our realtor, and the first house we see seems to be the right one. I'm surprised when Dan suggests we pray about it when we see it again and make an offer. Someone else has already signed a contract, but their financing appeared to be falling through. So we're disappointed when we find out they got the house after all. Did God answer our prayer with a "no?"

Dan's still at work, but I'm looking at a house our realtor found at the last minute. It's a "spec" home on a corner lot, brand new, and within our price range. As soon as I see it, I feel that it's perfect for us, and just know that he'll like it too. When Dan walks in the front door of the house the next day, he knows that it is the one, even before he sees the rest of it! This northern style "raised ranch" suits our tastes and lifestyle. The top half is cedar and the bottom is cement/block/stucco (CBS). It's nice to have a two-car garage.

*A few years later we buy the other corner lot. This gives us endless possibilities with the extra property. Through the years we build a basketball court in the backyard, add on a country-style screened-in porch, above-the-ground pool and two sheds. (We raised racing pigeons in one of the sheds for a few years). This home is truly from the Lord.*

God's financial intervention was again demonstrated through the relatively quick sale of my older, much smaller house, and the sizeable down payment we were able to put on our new home.

*Though we've both been blessed with all these things, I've discovered that what really matters is the people in my life, and especially my husband. Through the years I see, in increasing measure, how Dan is such a good man of integrity and a deeply sincere Christian. He has a servant's heart, and acts that out in many ways to me, neighbors and other acquaintances. Our marriage is not perfect, but our commitment and love for each other never waver. I know he is God's choice for me, and each year I come to love and appreciate him even more.*

Huggie doesn't move with us. While I was dating Dan, she became a lot less friendly to me and sometimes would bite my ankles or swat at me when I tried to pet her. Apparently she was jealous. We soon discovered an out-of-control flea problem, so we gave her to an animal shelter months before we moved. It's as though she was just with me to fill the loneliness and now her time with me was over!

# A Ready-Made Family

*"God sets the lonely in families."* (Psalm 68:6)

I never dreamed that I'd marry into a wonderful family of five grown children and two grandchildren on my wedding day! It amazes me to be called Grandma, when I'm only 38 and have never given birth. Through the years I am blessed to know each one of my new family better. All of Dan's sons and daughters and their spouses love me and I love them dearly. I couldn't ask for a better extended family to be part of.

Dan and I have spent many vacations in Indiana with his two sons Dan and Jeff and their families, as well as his Mom, brother and sisters. We've also vacationed in Tallahassee, where daughter Kim lived with her family until their recent move to Tennessee. Dan's daughter Janice lives in North Fort Myers and we see her and her family often.

Tony, Dan's son, was living in Indiana when we got married, but moved back to Florida a few years later. He now lives across the bridge in Cape Coral, and we get together when we can. When their four kids were little, we would have everyone over for Thanksgiving dinner and play basketball on the court Dan made in our backyard. A few times, some of the kids came for a sleepover. Now they're married and have babies of their own. At this writing, we have ten grandchildren and six great-grandchildren.

My own family, small to begin with, has dwindled down to only a few people. My sister Judy is my closest relative, along with her husband Ken and daughter Jenny. I keep in touch with a few cousins who live out of town and one aunt and uncle who are still living. That's about it, so I'm glad to be part of a larger family. God truly did "set the lonely in families" for me!

# A New Chapter in Our Marriage

It's the new millennium now, and 6 months after the year turns 2000, Dan retires form Ford. Not one to be idle, he's started a lawn service business. I like our arrangement: he does the heavy labor and I do the books! As we're doing the initial planning, Jim Dickinson, one of our FAA staff, designs a logo for us. We're looking very professional on the job and on paper.

For a short time, Dan provides lawn service for both RSW and Page Field Towers and their radar site. I'm still working then, and wave at him through the window when he passes by. The FAA has become a family affair. A few of the Tower people have come to our church. It's so good to see all the connections that have come about.

Dan develops an impressive clientele in our neighborhood, and we both have some special friendships with some of his customers. His excellent work and attention to detail spread his great reputation to the point where he has to turn down new clients. His compassionate heart is noticed and appreciated. This is his second calling in life.

*I believe God intervened in Dan's mind, to give him wisdom regarding when to retire from Ford, and what direction to pursue next. God guided us both in the mechanics of starting up this business, which has turned out to be a blessing to us and his clients.*

# Divine Intervention in the Library

## I'm Learning to Let Him Decide How to Use It

*"For we are God's workmanship, created in Christ Jesus to do good works, which God prepared in advance for us."* (Ephesians 2:10)

### 2002 – Present
### Changes and Challenges

Big changes are in store for our church! After much prayer and putting out a fleece, we, as a church body, have voted to move to another location. I am excited, along with everyone else, at this major undertaking, which we all sense God is leading us toward. We've bought the property, and have a collective vision of the church reaching out to this particular neighborhood. The building complex will house a sanctuary which can be instantly converted to a gym, yet be a beautiful place of worship on Sundays. The plans look great. One of the first agenda items will be to plan and host the community's Upward Basketball program in our new facility.

Pastor Brummett has given me the best gift - a large room for the library, right opposite the sanctuary. I am thrilled when a church member offers to build shelves on three of the four walls of my room, ceiling to floor, to house our 4,000 books and multi-media section.

After the construction begins, I occasionally drop in to picture everything in my mind.

Amazingly, we've already sold the old church to a church group that has their main service in the evening; so we can still worship there on Sunday mornings. In the meantime, the church office is renting space nearby.

It's then that I feel it's time to convert my still-handwritten catalog into a Book Librarian program on a computer the church has given me. This is a huge project, but since I'm retired, I have time to do it. At the end of each session, I faithfully back up the data. After many months, I can see the light at the end of the tunnel. It will be a great asset to me and anyone trying to find a book by title, subject or author.

Finally, the day arrives when we can start working in our respective new rooms. At first, I just sit there, amazed. The room is beautiful, with two windows on one side, and an additional one on another wall. There's a round table with chairs and a church member has donated a comfortable sofa. Dan and I have bought a nice desk to complete the furnishing of this room. Most of the books are still in storage, so Dan and I haul them in.

## Upgrades and Hard Work

Wow, this is a huge project! As I unpack the books, I'm thinking I might as well do this up right, like a public library. I've already classified the books according to Dewey Decimal numbers, so I type and affix labels on the book spines and label the shelves by category. This takes me a year and a half, but it is a thrill to see it all fall into place. It is so worth the hard work!

Our multi-media section contains good family movies and other videos and DVD's. We will soon have "Sunday Night at the Movies" at church. The various ministries of the church will also use the library from time to time. This lovely room will be getting a lot of good use.

As I've been working, I kind of meditate at the same time on what the library is really about, and what I want to accomplish. I've written and framed a purpose statement. I want this place of grace and peace to encourage, inspire, entertain and educate each person who comes in. I also want the library to extend beyond our own church, to reach the hurting, those searching to know God better; whatever God wants it to be. I've got lots of ideas spinning around in my mind, but don't know how to carry them out yet. I pray about it.

# Disaster Strikes

I've received some book donations and am at the church, ready to type in the catalog entries. Nothing happens. My computer is blank. It is dead. No one can bring it back to life. I am devastated at first; then I remember that I've backed it up faithfully on a disk. I go home feeling a little better, but not totally relieved.

This morning I'm feeling refreshed and hopeful that the computer tech will be able to restore everything like it was. My phone rings. I don't want to believe what I'm hearing now; the backup disk is <u>blank!</u> So all this time, that computer progress bar was lying to me when it said I was backed up! I am way beyond upset. My emotions are having a field day.

I'm frantically looking for some hope of retrieving those entries. Suddenly I receive some good news; about half of the 4,000 entries were saved on the church's networking system. That's not so bad, I guess; at least I have 2,000 entries. But now I realize that I don't know which ones are missing from my typed catalog, so there's no way around it. I'll have to do a complete book check from computer to shelf. This will not be a quick fix by any means. I have a friend who helps me in the library some, but this particular project is best done by one person. Guess I'll be busy for a very long time.

It takes a lot for me to get really angry, but as the full impact of this hits me, this is one of those times. To think of all my time and energy wasted! What looms ahead is a massive project, almost starting from scratch, again. It's not like I'm getting paid to do this, you know? My mind starts placing blame with thoughts of what should have been, but the Lord suddenly interrupts my thinking and attitude. I can't ignore His prompting to forgive whatever, or whoever (including me) caused this to happen.

As I pray, the Lord reminds me that I'm working for Him, not me. The library is not really about me. I gulp and ask His forgiveness for a resentful and pitying attitude. Soon I begin to see this event as an opportunity to verify each individual book on the shelf, and delete entries of lost books. By this time, it's been years since each book was totally accounted for.

I've learned that anger is not a sin if it brings to my attention some unconscious or unhealthy attitude that needs work. God reminds me that it's okay to be human, changes my thinking, and with His help I move on.

I'm also thankful that this happened at a season of my life when I actually had the time to do all that work. I can see good coming out of this 'disaster', because I really needed to expand the information on some of the books and tweak other entries in my catalog program.

Also, this was the second time my computer had crashed, and prompted a loving friend from church to buy a brand new computer for the library!

All of these things I see as God's timing.

## My Dreams of Library Outreach

I've been thinking of ways to use the library beyond just our own church people. Maybe a mobile library to visit shut-ins or nursing homes? What about having a 'Library Day' during the week and advertise it for neighbors to come? Nothing I try seems to work. Guess I have to leave this in the Lord's hands.

Community Bible Study has been meeting in our church building and I've decided to open our library to them. Our Teaching Director is thrilled, and several of the ladies there have been using the Library regularly. One of the "core groups" from CBS meets in the library when we break into groups of about 12 for discussion. They enjoy just being in that atmosphere. I'm so thankful that the Lord is using even the room itself as a place of peace and His Presence.

I've gotten a lot of book donations, and can't use all of them. Now the Lord is using our library to help a new, satellite church establish their own. The pastor is grateful to receive these books; I'm happy to have the extra space! Wow, God's been using me to set up libraries. Who'd have thought He'd lead me in that direction?!

*One day as I'm finishing up cataloging books at church, something wonderful happens to me. I'm sitting quietly, taking a breather before I pack up and suddenly I feel the most wonderful quiet joy and peace. It's like the Lord is smiling on me, and I feel His Presence so strongly. It's almost a surreal moment. Even this, I believe, is Divine intervention.*

# Outside My Comfort Zone

Why is it that every time I start to feel comfortable, somebody stirs the waters for me? Now I find myself being persuaded, though I have to admit gently, into planning a "Mitford Tea" library event for the ladies of the church. Many of my library patrons are excitedly reading Jan Karon's Mitford book series. The Tea idea has been mentioned more than once to me, so I'm seriously thinking about it. Organizing a social event is not my "cup of tea", but it's obvious to me that no one wants to head this up. I guess I'm volunteered. Is this God's intervention? Could be; it seems like this event should happen. It's good publicity for the library, too.

I'm feeling overwhelmed, not knowing where to start, but a few of the ladies assist me with the details. We decide on a pot-luck lunch which includes some recipes from Jan Karon's Mitford Cookbook. One of the ladies bakes the famous and delicious orange marmalade cake. Yummy! And of course, we have all kinds of hot and cold tea. We have some entertainment, even a last-minute fashion show that someone pleasantly surprises me with. The 40 women who attend are an enthusiastic group. Despite some snags and my nerves, they tell me they had a good time. I'm glad it went well, but I sure don't want to make a habit of it!

∼

While I'm recovering from this drain on my mind and emotions, someone else from church asks me to consider starting a book discussion club. I don't know about this. It does interest me, though, and I give it a lot of thought and prayer - this time over many months.

I can't say that I ever got a strong prompting from the Lord, but I don't sense a closed door either. Six people have signed the interest sheet I've posted on the bulletin board at church. I guess that's enough to give it a try.

We meet once a month – in the church library of course, read a selected book and then discuss it. I don't know, it just seems to be lacking something. I can't put my finger on it. For a few months, only two or three show up. It never really gets off the ground, so we disband after six months. Maybe it wasn't God's plan. At least I gave it a try, in case it was.

~

Now what? The library is running itself; is there something else I can do in this ministry? I pray some more and this time it's me with the idea – a book fair! I need to sell or give away books I no longer need, to make room for new ones. By now I have over a hundred excess or outdated books that I really don't want to throw away. As I chew on this awhile, I decide to go ahead and schedule it on a Saturday at the church. My helpers and I decide to just ask for donations and offer the books at no cost. Several people help me set up the books on long tables, and we plan refreshments and displays. I advertise the event in the newspaper and on Christian radio. I am working very hard on this project.

The big day has arrived, and here I am, along with a few helpers. The clock is ticking in a pretty quiet room. Is anyone going to show up? The hours of the fair are 10 – 4. After 11 a.m. some people come, and a few trickle in from time to time. The few who attend take lots of books and give generously.

I'm really disappointed the turnout was so low. In my eyes, this event was a bust! Well, maybe it was a success after all, because one person gave a large donation, and amazingly, almost all the books were taken!

Did God tell me to do the book fair? Maybe. I was glad to clear out the older books and to have more money to buy new ones.

*I'm learning that not every endeavor I set off on leads to a wildly successful conclusion, and that's okay. I have also learned that when God initiates something, it will succeed. I'm beginning to see the difference.*

But I keep getting lots of book donations! Many are duplicates, many are outdated. What do I do with them now? I bought a book cart to help me move books back when the church moved. Why not use it to offer free books to anyone who comes into the church?

I've made the book cart available at the free pain clinic which meets here on Tuesday nights. This is what I'm talking about! Many of the people coming in are unchurched, or have just found the Lord through our pain clinic counselors. Another God intervention in my Library plans, that I wouldn't have thought of on my own.

*In thinking about a 'calling,' I've observed that God didn't ask me to do something I was unsuited for, or would hate to do, or dread. Where did I get this idea that God's will is to make me miserable? I'm learning that God smiles when He sees that serving Him brings me pleasure.*

*I've learned that a calling is not necessarily something 'big' in the world's view of importance or even how many people are impacted. It's simply God's plan for my life, and what He knows He can do through me. I've discovered that sometimes God calls* us to do something for only a season, or even just once. Not everything has to make perfect sense.

I've always known that I take myself way too seriously. But lately, I've realized that God really enjoys a good laugh or two. See if you agree....

# Buffaloes and Cell Phones

## God's Sense of Humor and Personal Involvement

*"A cheerful heart is good medicine, but a crushed spirit dries up the bones."* (Proverbs 17:22)

### Buffalo Betty
### Sometime in the 1990's

It's National Secretaries' Week. My bosses have plans to take me to lunch, probably on Secretaries' Day, this Wednesday. Just like they've done each year.

The phone rings and an unfamiliar voice asks for me by name.

"Hi, Betty, this is Babcock Wilderness Center. We were having a raffle at our place and are pleased to tell you that you are the winner," he happily states.

"Oh, how did that happen?" I ask. "It seems a long time ago that Dan and I were there."

"Well, how long ago were you there?" he asks, seriously.

"Oh, over a year ago," I respond, wondering what is going on. We'd really enjoyed this open-air bus adventure, but I don't remember a raffle, though we'd signed a required waiver, since some animals roam free.

"Well, we took people who visited us over the past 24 months, and drew your name. You're not going to believe what you won," he says with a smile and building excitement in his voice.

"What's that?" I ask, still not suspecting anything (though their use of the wrong name – Babcock Wilderness *Center* instead of Babcock Wilderness *Adventures* should have tipped me off).

"We were raffling off one of our buffaloes to help out the wilderness center," he says (with some unique buffalo sounds in the background).

**"So you have won a buffalo!"**

"Aw, come on," I burst out laughing as I say this – while my mind is trying to decide if I can believe him. But I don't think on my feet that fast.

"I'm serious," he says, in a smiling, but matter-of-fact voice.

"What do I do with it?" I ask, still laughing, but totally confused.

"Just about anything you want to, really, it's yours." He says, with what I imagine to be a straight face.

"Well, I don't have any place to put it" I state flatly, though still wondering if this is really happening.

"You don't? Well, we take care of the delivery; we bring it right to your house and give you the food supply for the first two months to set you up and everything."

"No, I don't think that's possible" I say, still laughing. "You know it's just a, you know, a house." *What on earth??*

"You have a yard out back, or anything?"

"Oh, yeah." I hesitate a second then laughingly ask, "Is it a baby?"

"No, it's a full grown one. Would a baby be okay?" he asks, leading me on.

"Uh, no," I answer, still giggling, "my husband would never permit it."

"What am I going to do now?" he asks. "Maybe I should tell you that you're being joked upon by Ron."

The man on the phone is a disk jockey for a local rock station, and amidst his own laughter tells me that I'm the recipient of a practical joke as part of a Secretaries' Week contest for the best joke played on your secretary. While he's telling me this, Ron is laughing hysterically, and comes out of hiding to confess. I'm sure my face is beet red, but I have to laugh at myself. Ron is one of the staff people I work for. He's a good friend and loves to play practical jokes. He got me good on this one!

A few days later the radio station calls to tell me that with over 240 entries, I won the contest as the funniest! They play the spot live on the radio, along with the practical joke pre-recorded segment. They tell me I was a very good sport. The next day, I'm presented with a gorgeous vase of flowers and dinner for two at a restaurant on Fort Myers Beach.

I think this was maybe part of God's intervention to remind me to lighten up at my workplace. I've been told that I work too hard. God's reminded me that His burden is light and wants me to live more lightly - a concept my nature has a hard time grasping at times.

*At my retirement party in 2002, Ron reads a very sweet, touching framed poem that he wrote for me. As I begin to well up at the sentiment, he reads the last line: "Your buffalo stepped on my foot!" That saves the day for me; the threatened floodgate of tears is kept at bay, and the laughter keeps me from feeling too sad about leaving my co-workers of 20 years.*

# An Interesting Trip

Every February, our small administrative staff drives up to our Tampa Tower Hub for Black History Month events. I don't like to drive, and hitch a ride with whoever is willing to take his own car. Usually, all the cars from our reduced fleet of Government vehicles are in use.

This particular time, my boss is driving. Since he lives nearby, he picks me up from my home. A supervisor is already in the passenger seat, so I'm gratefully sitting in the back.

I'd prayed the night before and in the morning that God would keep us safe, telling Him my concerns about my boss's habit of constantly talking on his cell phone, especially while driving. This is before texting comes to cell phones, but it still makes me nervous.

We leave my house around 7:00 a.m. The trip takes a little over two hours, and on the way, he stops for coffee and to top off the gas tank. He returns to the car and tells us,

"My cell phone isn't getting a signal; that's strange; we're still in good range."

He tries again while driving, and nothing. He's getting very exasperated and wonders what's going on. We stop a few more times, and each time we watch him waving his phone around outside, but with the same result. I'm starting to think that this is more than a coincidence, and find it amusing. I'm trying to suppress imminent laughter.

My boss calls his phone carrier from the Tampa Office as soon as we arrive there. The carrier says that everything checks out okay on their end. We spend several hours at Tampa Tower, and then stop for a late lunch on the way back to Fort Myers.

All through the uneventful ride back home, the cell phone is unresponsive on the occasional attempts he makes. My boss drops me off at my house around 6:00 p.m. I happily tell Dan about my safe and cell phone-free trip.

The next morning as I arrive at work, my boss, looking very perplexed, tells me:

"The strangest thing happened; as soon as I pulled out of your driveway, my cell phone worked again!"

I just smile, and enjoy my little secret. I can't wait to tell Dan the rest of the story. Is God awesome, or what?

*Not only did God protect me; He showed me the humor in it. Nothing is too small for God. Somehow I think He got a kick out of doing this for me. Didn't a sense of humor originate with Him?*

# The Missing Cell Phone

## 2010

My husband Dan has been working at a friend's house, helping him clear leaves off his roof. He is aware that his cell phone (a Tracfone) has dropped to the ground, but neither he nor his friend can find it. After a long and fruitless search, he asks me to call his number, thinking the phone will ring and guide them to it. Nothing happens, so they finally give up looking, and Dan buys a new cell phone. The missing one was old, anyway. Too bad the pre-paid minutes on his old Tracfone are lost, so we think.

About a week later, Dan is back working in their yard and there in the grass in plain sight is the phone! It had rained heavily during that week, but miraculously the phone still works. I've had cell phones which were permanently damaged by less water than that.

So what do we need a third phone for? At the time the phone is found, my father has just begun living in a nursing home. He does not have a phone in the room, and the one phone on his wing is rarely available to receive calls. The recovered phone, with its minutes, is a blessing. My sister can call our Dad from Jacksonville, and she often pre-plans the time so Dad can have the phone within reach. It also comes in handy when I'm there to help Dad place a call to Judy, or to update her right from the nursing home on any changes in his condition. This phone is very simple, without extra features that would confuse him. He can use it pretty easily.

When Dad is no longer at the nursing home and I come to collect his personal possessions, the phone is missing. We search diligently and again, try to locate it by calling the number. It's nowhere to be found. It could have been misplaced or stolen by someone at the nursing home. Guess we'll never know. There weren't a lot of minutes left on it.

How ironic: I wonder if it's Divine intervention that the phone was available only for that time and purpose. When we found the phone the first time, it had a lot of minutes remaining on it, so it didn't cost Dad anything for quite some time – a help in Dad's meager finances. You may consider this a small thing, but I like to think that God surprises us with blessings of all sizes.

In retrospect I see that the lighter times prepare you for the harder ones. In my subconscious mind, I vaguely know I am going to have to deal with something very difficult, and soon.

# Dad's Rescues and Amazing Grace

## Divine Interventions for us Both

*"But He said to me, 'My grace is sufficient for you, for My power is made perfect in weakness."* (2 Corinthians 12:9)

### 1986-2001

My Dad, I joke, should hang a "Doctor is In" shingle outside his home. Dad took extremely good care of Mom all those years. He learned a lot in the medical field, taking her to countless doctors and hospitals. While still able to, Mom taught him how to take care of all the financial tasks she always did. This was very valuable to him as her cancer progressed.

A few months after Mom's death in 1986, I notice Dad becoming friendlier with an old acquaintance from their very distant New York past. Emeline was actually the wife of Dad's best friend, way back when. Her husband died at an early age, leaving her to raise four adopted children alone in New York and then Ohio. Now they're all adults, and one of her sons lives in Fort Myers. She decided to move to Florida a few years ago, and reconnected with Dad and Mom through the church.

I can see that Emeline has her eyes set on Dad, and he doesn't seem to mind a bit. They start dating and my quiet, reserved 69-year old father is soon acting like a goofy teenager. My emotions are in a turmoil. She isn't at all like my sweet Mom and in my thinking, it's just way too soon! I feel kind of heart sick and pray. I think God reminds me that Dad's grieving over Mom started a long time before her death, as he suffered right along with her for nine years. I begin to see that it's good he is willing to move on with his life. He knows Mom is in Heaven and so do I. We'll see what happens; not really anything I can do about it anyway. Surely they're just friends at this point.

Wow, I've never seen Dad like this. He's quite smitten. Yet I'm still not prepared when they sit me down to talk when I'm over at his house.

"You know your Dad and I have been spending a lot of time together," Emeline begins.

"We love each other and are planning to get married. I don't know how you feel about this, but we really do want your blessing." Dad looks a little tentative about my reaction, but I can see that he's happy.

I had an inkling this was coming, so it's not a total shock. But the timing is. It's only been four months. Though my mind says, "No, it's way too soon!" I send up a quick prayer for grace and find myself saying, amidst my pain,

"Honestly, it's kind of hard so soon after losing Mom, but I want you both to be happy, and can see that you are." I wish them the best, though my heart's not in it.

Dad and Emeline are married the last week of July 1986, in Ohio, where her other sons and families live. They have a short honeymoon and the two of them move into Dad's house when they get back to Fort Myers. It's a very strange feeling when I'm over there. So much of Mom still lingers in that house, now occupied by my step-mother. I don't think I'll ever get used to that.

I can see, though, that Dad is happy. They have some really good years, traveling and having fun. They go on a church Work and Witness trip to Australia and New Zealand and on the way back, vacation in Hawaii. This is a brand new world for Dad, and I'm happy for that addition to his life.

Twelve years later, Dad is again caring for a sick wife. Emeline's health deteriorates over several years. These years are very tough for all members of our family and Emeline's. Dad and I bond as we deal with some extremely difficult issues. Emeline passes away in 2002, just a few months before I retire.

## Alone Again
## 2002

Dad's life has changed so much in the past decade! The one constant in his life has been his home. He's lived in the same house since 1980. It's a comfortable home for him, and very close to the shopping he needs to do. Dan and I are less than 20 minutes away, so at least I'm close by.

I remember that as I approached my retirement date, I told the Lord that I want to take care of Dad now that I'll have more time, and want to get to really know him. Mom was always the dominant personality in our family, and I never felt all that close to my father. Little do I know how much closer I'll soon be involved in his life.

For several years, he functions well on his own, and comes every weekend to visit and share a meal with us. I am blessed to have the two most important men in my life together, just enjoying each other in simple, easy ways. We often watch golf together on TV. Dan set up a homemade putt–putt green on our basketball court in the yard and he and Dad putter around. Sometimes I join in also. It's fun and relaxing.

## 2007

The day Dad turns 90 is a happy day! He doesn't like being around a lot of people, so we have a small gathering of his closest friends and Pastor Brummett and Linda at my home to celebrate. It's a sweet time, going down memory lane. I made a poster of family photos and show it and the roots album Mom made to our guests.

# An Interrupted Vacation

## 2009

Dad's health and mobility are not too bad for his age, and he is agreeable to Dan and me driving to Indiana for our annual vacation. I coordinate with friends and the church in the event he would need assistance. He still does pretty well fending for himself, so I stock up ahead of time for his food and other emergency supplies. He's got a list of numbers to call for every situation I can think of.

We usually complete the 1200-mile drive to Kokomo in two days. Early in the morning on the second day, my cell phone wakes me up in our motel room. It's Janice, Dan's daughter. Dad fell at home and broke his shoulder. He's in pretty bad shape.

Our friend Gregg, who lives near Dad, called 911 and the hospital treated Dad's wounds but sent him back home. I call Gregg and find out that Dad really needs to get back to the hospital; he's totally helpless and needs more medical attention than we could provide. But the hospital won't accept him! Gregg and his wife Cheryl stay with him, while we drive the nearly 600 miles back home.

I call Dad's doctor and she shames the hospital into taking Dad back. He ends up staying there for several days, and then is sent to a rehab center.

While Dad's shoulder is healing, the physical therapists work with him to build his leg strength. I can't say enough about the quality of care that he receives from every physical therapist. They are incredibly efficient and compassionate people. When his shoulder heals he has more therapy, and eventual occupational therapy to get him in condition to return to his home. I am so grateful for these people who don't shortchange such an elderly and frail man from these benefits. These people work wonders!

Dad stays at the rehab center as long as Medicare and his insurance will cover it. They do an in-home evaluation and clear him to go home.

I thank God for making something good result from this fall in that Dad regained a lot of the strength he had lost over the past two years. Dad's life was getting back on track a little.

# Helping Dad

Life begins to change when Dad falls a few more times over the next few years. He can no longer drive and soon will give his car to a needy person through our church. His former 5'10" frame is bent almost in two from his extremely curved spine. He just clears my 5'2" height.

My care for Dad intensifies. I do all his food shopping and errands. He rarely leaves his house, except for church and doctor appointments. I'm glad for these times when I can give back, though sometimes I just wish I didn't have to be 'on call' all the time.

I've never felt comfortable in hospitals, doctors' offices and other medically-related surroundings. I give God the credit for giving me strength for doing what is still not easy for me to deal with. The graphic reality of some of Dad's medical conditions requires extra grace from God for both of us.

But life has its sweet moments, too. Dad lives close to the church, so every Sunday I pick him up between Sunday School and church times. Sitting between my father and husband at church is a privilege. On Fathers' Day, Dad won a huge apple pie at church for being the oldest father, just months after his 92nd birthday. He was thrilled to be recognized and loved. The pie is good, too!

How quickly life can change. The next day, Dad literally crawls to the phone to tell me he's fallen and can't get up. This begins a series of trips to hospitals and rehab centers over several monthly intervals. Amazingly, he bounces back each time, still able to live in his beloved home. Each episode lasts longer, though. Dad's attitude of 'going with the flow' helps him through each hospital or rehab experience, though there are many negative, tough experiences along the way. God, of course, is his greatest Helper.

I start feeling emotional pain at the thought of Dad's old age. I don't want to lose him, and that possibility is frequently coming to my mind. I pray that he won't be afraid when his time comes. He doesn't want to discuss it. One day when he's in the right mood, we discuss his end-of-life preference. This helps me a bit.

# A Horrible Scare

Dad and I have a routine that works quite well. I either go there or call him at certain times of the day. I am now calling him repeatedly. He's not answering. He's probably in the shower or bathroom. I don't worry until my third call. This doesn't sound right. I find Dan working in the backyard.

"Dan, I think something's happened to Dad. I've called him repeatedly; I have a bad feeling about this. I'm going over there."

"Okay, call if you need me. Remember, we've had scares before. It might not be as bad as it seems. I'll be here."

It comforts me to know that Dan will come right over if I call. I leave a message on Dad's answer machine that I'm on the way. I'm in a panic as I drive, not knowing what I'm going to find. Worst case scenarios are furiously playing out in my mind.

I first pray, "Lord, please give me supernatural strength and grace if he's not alive." I don't want to think of what it would be like to find him lifeless on the floor. Then I pray, "Lord, please keep Dad alive so Judy can come down from Jacksonville and see him one last time."

When I arrive, all is quiet as I make my way to the back of the house. As I enter his bedroom with foreboding trepidation, the first thing I see (and yes, you do live these events in slow motion) is his feet extended on the floor. A long second later, I see him propped up at the foot of his bed, smiling! He fell the night before and couldn't use his life alert button, having taken it off in the bathroom when washing his face. He was unable to move to the phone, and was immobilized on the floor for 18 hours! He could hear my message on his amplified phone so he knew I was coming.

My relief that he's alive calms me down enough to call 911. It takes three paramedics to get my frail 120 lb. father onto the stretcher because of his extreme pain and the curvature of his spine.

Dad's got a urinary tract infection, which severely affects elderly people, and caused his fall. He's fractured some ribs and a vertebra in his lower back. Amazingly, he eventually recovers his health and some of his strength, again at a rehab facility. They do a home evaluation after several months and clear him to live in his home once again. We've arranged for additional grab bars and railings to be installed throughout the house.

Moving in with us is out of the question. Most of the living area in our home is upstairs. By this time, Dad can't navigate our stairs at all. Also, he is very particular in the way he lives and doesn't want to leave his home. He and I both know that it would be a very uncomfortable and difficult situation for all of us. Besides, his home is part of what gets him up every morning, to face the day.

These falls and health issues are becoming more and more frequent. It preys on my mind almost constantly. I want to do what's best for Dad, but he has a very strong, independent streak and is very set in his ways. I guess I just have to take it one day at a time, like he does.

The fact that Dad's life was spared when he was immobile on the floor for 18 hours makes me conclude that it just wasn't his time yet. I believe God had a specific date and time for Dad's home-going to his heavenly home.

Because Dad worked under a federal system, he has very good health insurance. What a blessing to have his massive hospital and medical expenses totally covered. Again, I trace this back to Sunshine Biscuit's move which caused Dad to apply to work for the Post Office, through which he has this excellent medical coverage.

# The Struggles Intensify

Dad has one fall too many, and this is the beginning of his end-of-life struggle. He's had several episodes of pneumonia. We learn that he has had COPD for some time, but no one had told us. The worst news is that he has started aspirating food into his lungs. He eventually requires a feeding tube, and can no longer eat or drink anything by mouth. I feel so sad to see him unable to eat, hooked up to so many tubes and machines. I try to bury my own pain and be strong for him.

By now we've had to admit him to a nursing home. This is not what any of us want, but the only alternative. His income is in that in-between place, so I obtain legal and financial counsel to enable him to live there. God's intervention is now giving me the contacts I need, with practical advice and help in making many difficult decisions for Dad's care. These people were a tremendous help in all of these processes. The Lord also helps me explain everything to Dad, who can still comprehend most of this, though it's very complicated. His body may be wearing out, but he has the mind of a much younger man. That is a blessing I can't thank God enough for.

God's marvelous grace sustains Dad when he can't eat. He dreams about food and somehow that comforts him; he almost feels like he is eating. He likes to watch the Food Channel on TV. That's the last thing I'd want, if I was in his situation.

Dad's highly skilled speech therapist is the most wonderful blessing. (His speech is fine, but his swallowing muscles and esophagus aren't.) As I watch her work with Dad daily, I observe the tender way she treats him - as if he were her own father in the same situation.

If anyone could get those swallowing muscles to work, she could. But his 94-year-old body just isn't up to it. Dad is always alert and as accepting of his circumstances as humanly possible, with God's grace.

*Observing Dad's gentle, accepting spirit that comes from a quiet faith has been very inspirational to me. It demonstrated visibly the tremendous grace of God in utterly horrible situations. It also reminded me that God never promised us a pain-free life; but His grace and guidance are always here for us. I'm amazed.*

*Through all of these challenging and heart-breaking circumstances, I had to totally depend on God for His strength, wisdom and sometimes direct intervention. I recall times when leaving the nursing home, I'd just fall over my steering wheel and pray, "God I can't do this anymore!" But He came through and recharged me every time.*

# Judy and Dad

My sister comes at the critical times to help out. She lives in Jacksonville, a day-long trip, and can't come often because of family matters. The times she does come help me tremendously. One time she stayed at the hospital throughout the night, sleeping briefly in the chair.

Judy and Dad have grown closer over recent years, when she and her family moved back to Florida from the Pacific Coast. Judy's husband's job required numerous moves throughout the country, including several years in St. Petersburg, FL when Jenny was very young.

When Ken retired, God guided them to move back to Florida, not many years before Dad's health declined. This enabled Judy to make more trips here and surely was God's timing. She was also able to come celebrate Dad's 90th birthday with us in 2007. That was a happy time!

There were many physical episodes over the past two years when we thought this would be Dad's last. He would bounce back, regaining his strength enough for the rehab people to clear him once again to live at home. It gave Judy and me more time with him. Now she and Dad have some really precious times together in this last chapter of his life. I believe God arranged that.

# It's Time

Dad's last few months are very hard, but he is still in his right mind, all the way to his last breath, at 94 years old. It really helps me when our pastor comes and visits Dad in the hospital; this time it's a few weeks before his final days. Judy is there and we have a very happy, pleasant time, just enjoying each other and the Lord. We share some quiet laughter, and Dad smiles a lot while we're all together.

On Sunday, Judy offers to stay with him instead of going to church. She wants to make the most of their time together. Dad points his finger at her and says with a smile, "You go to church!" It reemphasizes Dad's priority in life, our Lord and God.

This is such a hard time for my sister and me. The uncertainty of his condition makes it difficult for her to know when to come, these past weeks. This last time, she had just gotten back home when she had to come back a day or two later. It's a long, arduous trip, amidst all the emotion of everything.

Now, a week or so later, Pastor Brummett comes again. Sensitive to something different going on, he asks Dad,

"Gene, I think you're like the Apostle Paul, torn between going to be with the Lord and staying here; but either is okay with you, is that right?"

Dad nods his head and says, "Yes." He looks to be at peace.

I'm about to 'lose it' and have to turn away. I know in my spirit that his time is short.

A few days later, the hospital physician tells me there's nothing else they can do. They've now pulled the feeding tube and are sending him to Hospice. At their suggestion, I check the facility out before they move him. What a wonderful place of tender, compassionate care! I wish they could have moved him there sooner. I tell Dad about it and he just nods. He knows what that means. They move him in the early evening, so I don't plan to go until the next morning. I've been with him all day.

# Home at Last

June 2, 2011, around 6:00 a.m., Hospice's call wakes me. Dad has started the dying process. I can come if I want to see him, but she's not sure he'll last. I decide to not make the trip. At 6:30 a.m. they call. He just took his last breath; he went peacefully.

Those first moments are so hard, and Dan and I comfort each other. I'm so glad I'm not alone in this. But my very next thought is that Dad is feasting on his favorite foods in Heaven. He loved God, lived a good life, and I am so thankful that I come from such good stock. I wouldn't wish him back to all that suffering.

Maybe having time to prepare for Dad's death helps, so I feel some relief – not just for him, but also that I no longer have to see the suffering. It's been so stressful going to hospitals and nursing homes day after day, though I never regretted a minute. Now I already miss him greatly!

Judy and I plan parts of the memorial service for Dad, which will be held at our church in a few days. I know of a local photo shop that can make a video of family photos for us. Judy and I bring a bunch of old slides, faded photos and other pictures to the shop; can they make all of this into a video? "No problem", she tells us. The finished product is beyond our expectations. It takes about 10 minutes to show, and we'll have it continuously running before the service begins.

I've recently heard a beautiful song, *"Knowing What I Know about Heaven"* (words & music by *Billy Austin/Dave Robbins/Sarah Darling)* sung by Guy Penrod on his *Breathe Deep* CD. I'd really like Brenda, our church's office manager, to sing it at Dad's service. It's such short notice, but I ask her anyway. She tells me she needs the accompaniment tape. Miraculously, she finds it at a local Christian bookstore and learns it in just two days!

The memorial service is so sweetly quiet and has a tender intimacy to it that is precious. I feel love pouring out to me from the pastors on the platform. Brenda sings my requested song beautifully and it means so much to me; especially the last line of the chorus that says, "*I could hope that I could pray you back, but why on earth would I do that, when you're somewhere life and love never end. Knowing what I know about Heaven.*"

# Final Things and Some Closure

## June 2 – October 1, 2011

Because of the necessary legal actions for Dad's care that we'd already done, just about everything financial is taken care of in record time. The legal pre-arrangements enable Judy and me to immediately put the house up for sale. With Dan's input, the three of us decide to try to sell it ourselves.

Even though we're in the middle of the downturn of the housing market, we have a number of people interested in this house. God must be in this again, as we sell it to a family who really need this particular house and location – in just four months! I'm so grateful for the closure this brings to help me heal and move on with my life.

## God's Gift to Me

Fast forward to May 2013. I'm putting back some photos I'd taken from albums to show my hair stylist. One photo is of Mom and me together. It turns out I am the exact same age now that she was in the picture, an interesting (but irrelevant) thought. I'm exhausted from filing paperwork all day in my home office and push back in my recliner, wanting to relax and read. No, I'm too tired to read, so I close my eyes and clear my mind.

*It's very quiet in the house and I feel at peace. Suddenly I actually <u>see</u> Mom and Dad, side by side and smiling at me – their brightly-shining faces radiant with joy! It lasts only a few seconds, but enough to be indelible in my mind. They look to be in their 30's or 40's and I see only their faces, but it's* *real and wonderful and a comfort. This is yet another of God's interventions to comfort me, even after all these years.*

~

God's interventions in my life include much more than this vision and the ways He's helped me cope. It's also the sweetness of His presence with me. When I remember to surrender everything to God, His peace breaks through. That is Divine intervention. However, I tend to forget this quite often. That causes me problems.

# Personal Struggles

## God Comes Through at My Lowest Point

*"I do not concern myself with great matters or things too wonderful for me. But I have stilled and quieted my soul; like a weaned child with its mother, like a weaned child is my soul within me."* (Psalm 131:1b-2)

All through my life I have had recurring periods of nervous problems which manifest physically. As a child and through my teens, I was always very thin. I remember Mom taking me to the ice cream parlor daily, trying to get me past 39 pounds (which was not normal for my age at the time). It bothered me that I always weighed about 10 pounds less than the smallest child in my class.

I remember throwing up regularly in third or fourth grade, while standing in line for the restroom at lunchtime. This was around the time we'd moved into that tiny apartment (having previously lived with my grandparents) and I had to change schools. I was very timid and anxious in social situations. My fourth grade teacher told Mom that I was much too serious for my age. In sixth grade I would often eat lunch at my uncle's house across the street from the school to avoid social stress. Although smart, I never wanted to speak up in class. Mom and Dad took me to doctors, but no lasting solutions were found.

I've had major self-esteem issues all through my life. Though our family was not overly affectionate, I have always known that my family loved me. We've been a very normal family - no abuse or cruelty of any kind. I never understood why I had this problem. Mom and Dad didn't either.

I was fortunate to have a few childhood friends to play with, but never felt comfortable with anyone whose personality didn't match mine. I always wanted to play it safe and didn't like to face new experiences.

Although I've been a Christian throughout my life, this hasn't eliminated the fear, insecurity and self-induced stress, with its resulting physical problems. While varying in frequency through the years, these episodes became more intense and lasted longer as I grew older. I went to doctors who prescribed all sorts of medications, none of which helped me.

I had six months of non-medical therapy with a Christian counseling organization in 1998 in the midst of another episode. I learned that my body is highly reactive to any kind of stress, both external and physical. A recommended book gave me clearer understanding about my physical symptoms and how they were connected to my thinking.

The sessions were most helpful in the way my counselor accepted me exactly as I was, not thinking I was weird or criticizing me for my lack of faith. The main conclusion I came to, though, was that this wretched 'monkey on my back' is something I will have to continue to learn to live with. At least I had a reason for why I react the way I do. I did improve eventually, as I had the other times.

*In retrospect, from what I know now, I believe the causes are genetic and chemical in nature. It's not necessary to place blame or analyze it to death. Over the past few years, I have discovered that this emotional makeup of my being is not something to be condemned or criticized for. It just is.*

# 2008-2011

This particular nervous episode, the longest yet, is probably brought on by Dad's physical aging problems and my responsibility for his well-being. I have terrible insomnia and progressive weight loss, even though I eat pretty well. I worry about my health and my imagination plays out various illnesses and worst-case scenarios. I've got to do something!

As I pray about this, I feel impressed to go to a gastro doctor. I remember the compassionate doctor who did Dan's routine colonoscopy a few years ago. I find the phone number and get over my first hurdle by making the appointment. With my nerves so bad, I dread setting foot in any doctor's office, but here I am. The doctor is very nice, but right away senses that I need to see a psychiatrist. But to be on the safe side, he takes the usual tests (which accelerate my stress even more). Everything checks out okay. I am very impressed by this doctor's caring manner. He has a calming effect on me.

But psychiatry is not what I want; it's a blow to my ego. The doctor understands this, but insists that I keep his list of the top three recommended psychiatrists. When I start to feel a little better, knowing there's nothing physically wrong with me, I just file the list away.

During this time, I've been attending Community Bible Study, which is held on Wednesday mornings at my church. It's interdenominational and very spiritual. I feel loved, accepted and cared for. One dear person from CBS takes me under her wing. She calls me every week and we speak for an hour or so. Not only does she pray for me and listen, she also gives me helpful, practical advice.

Some time passes and a new doctor is brought to my attention. He focuses on natural healing. I wonder if he might help me with my digestive problems, weight loss and insomnia. I've never had much success with natural medicine or health food diets, though. One day, out of sheer desperation, I call his office and the line just keeps on ringing. The next time I call, I get a recording and leave a message. I never hear from them again. I believe this is God's intervention.

In the meantime, my friend from CBS calls and I learn that her daughter had gone to the same digestive health doctor I did. The conversation then evolves to her telling me that her other daughter is seeing a wonderful psychiatrist, who helps her greatly. I dig out the list I'd been given and her daughter's doctor is the top one recommended! I call immediately and have an appointment a few days later.

~

I know this doctor is absolutely the right fit for me. Even walking into his office brings me into an atmosphere of peace. He has made a world of difference with medication he has precisely adapted to my super-sensitive-to-drugs body, and his counseling has been effective and encouraging. I eat and sleep well and have gained all of my weight back. He also encourages my faith and sometimes incorporates it into the counseling.

I can't really describe what he's said to me that's made a difference. Most of what he tells me I've already known, but it's the way everything fits together, I guess, which helps me leave his office knowing I'm better for it. There's no magic formula, although he's given me some tools to help me when panic attacks seem to be coming on, or to help me de-stress. Yes, my body continues to react to stress more than most people, but I can cope much better now. I continue to see my psychiatrist several times a year, which I consider to be maintenance visits.

I've learned and experienced that God used friends to help me find people who could help me, when my friends couldn't. I am so grateful for this friend from CBS and also my faithful friend, Ruth Sedockin, who has been my prayer partner and phone buddy for over 25 years. They both listen, encourage and at times give me food for thought.

God closed the doors I'd tried to open: Even if I had selected a psychiatrist from the list of three, I would have chosen a different doctor. God knew who could help me the most.

God removed the guilt and shame I'd carried around most of my life for being an anxious person. I have also learned that going to a doctor of any kind is not a sign of weak faith. God often uses earthly resources to help us all.

Most importantly, God gave me a husband who stuck with me through all of my hardest times and episodes, and still does when things come up from time to time.

God continues to give me scriptures to help me through emotionally tough situations which sometimes occur. Staying grounded in the Bible is vital. I just needed something more to incorporate and apply God's truth into my thoughts and daily living. My psychiatrist has helped me with that. I still have issues that affect me, but the reactions are much less intense.

# I Can See Clearly Now

## God's Guidance and Confirmation

*"The Lord will guide you always."* (Isaiah 58:11a)

My eyesight is more complicated than most people's. From early childhood, I've been highly myopic, wearing coke-bottle glasses until technology in later years thinned them out. I also have a good degree of astigmatism, glaucoma, dry eye and need glasses to read. I wore contacts for about ten years, but the dry eye made them stick and frequently come out of my eye.

Over the past few years, I've developed cataracts in both eyes. A year ago, I thought I was ready to schedule cataract surgery with the ophthalmologist I've gone to for many years. I don't like the idea of someone cutting my eye, but my vision was getting less correctable, so we both agreed it was time. I hadn't made the appointment yet when I started having a lot of pain in my hip, and ended up having MRI's and a complete body scan. This was enough for me to cope with at the time (It turned out to be arthritis, and improved tremendously with a cortisone shot). I felt that I could postpone the eye surgery for another year, and had new lenses made for my eyeglasses, which improved my vision some. I was still legal to drive.

201

## September 2013

As another year approaches, I realize that this is the time and place to start making preparations for the cataract surgery. Although my doctor is a true professional with a very good reputation, there have been little things from time to time – little "yellow flags" which make me wonder if the outlined plans and procedures are right for me. The doctor did answer all of my questions to my satisfaction, so I'm thinking my hesitant feelings are coming from my anxious nature. I see no real reason to not go ahead with this doctor and I take a deep breath and make all the appointments.

When I get home, I re-read all the materials, think and pray. Although the still-lingering uneasiness is minimal, I feel led to call a knowledgeable optician I trust to help guide my thoughts. He talks to me for a long time, sharing a lot of his knowledge with me and suggests that I get a second opinion. He recommends another ophthalmologist, and after talking it over with Dan, I make an appointment.

On Sunday, our pastor mentions in his morning prayer that God will provide wisdom for those seeking to make the right decision. This, like the prayer in Lakeland years ago for a job, confirms and reminds me that God truly does guide my circumstances and me.

A friend at church stops in the church library to chat and I share my situation with her. Before I tell her the name of the recommended eye doctor, she enthusiastically tells me how much she and her husband like theirs – the very same ophthalmologist I'm to see the next day!

~

I can tell right away that this doctor is going to be a good one. After his examination he <u>sits down</u> to talk with me, like he's got all the time in the world. He explains things clearly and has a slightly different solution, which we both believe is better suited for my particular situation. Halfway through this visit, I feel myself relaxing a little, and sense an assurance that I didn't have before.

The fact that he sat down is significant to me, because it's unusual in my experience with the medical field. Most doctors, while standing, will ask if I have any questions but seem to not encourage anything but a quick question. I feel that this doctor is coming down to my level, is interested in me as a person, and not in a rush. I sense that he is humble and caring, encouraging questions while being knowledgeable and efficient at what he does.

In a previous chapter, I quoted a scripture verse which says that we're seated with Christ in heavenly places. Hebrews 12:2 tells us that Christ is seated at the right hand of God. Being seated is a peaceful inner condition, the work having already been done (as Christ's sacrifice for our sins, for example). So when I pray, I can be seated **with** Christ, knowing He's heard my prayer and has me covered. Jesus is making intercession for me. It is very comforting for me to know He is not in a frenzy or overly busy in solving my perplexing problems. I need to remind myself of that.

And not only that, God again intervened for me, unexpectedly. Just a week before the surgery, a member of my Community Bible Study group, whom I didn't know is an optician, talked with me at length about my choices and understood my particular eye situation. She confirmed that I'd made the right decision. I don't believe her being in my group of 12 people was a coincidence.

# New Eyes!

## October 2013 – December 2013

The surgeries have gone well, though my highly sensitive body and emotions have had a workout. Despite all the confirmations and assurances, I approached the surgeries with my natural reaction of fear. But you know what? God was with me right through my feelings of anxiety and my off-the-charts adrenalin.

An amazing thing happened while I was waiting in pre-op. I was hooked up to the heart monitor and could see the wild ups and downs on the screen. Trying to calm down seemed futile, until I whispered "Jesus" twice. Instantly, I saw those readings become what I think look like a normal, even heartbeat!

I am very grateful for the compassionate staff at the surgery center, and particularly for the anesthesiologist who took the time to discuss the options and the reasoning behind her decisions as she worked with my overly sensitive body.

I haven't had the usual instant thrill with my new eyes because I need eyeglasses for astigmatism, reading and a small distance correction. My vision during the two weeks between each eye's surgery is really off, because of my extreme myopia. But it's still a brand new world for me. I do have my first 'aha' moment when I take a shower and can actually see my individual toes! It's so nice to get up in the morning and be able to see without having to immediately reach for my glasses.

~

My eyes are now healed, and my eye-brain adjustment is bringing me into sharper focus each day. I'd compare my new vision correction to going from analog TV to digital high definition. Thank you, Lord, for my new eyes!

My new glasses are great, with the latest technology for transitions lenses which turn much darker outside and lighten or darken in increments. I'm amazed to find out that my lens implants have UV protection! I no longer need those big, clunky wrap-around sunglasses to wear over my regular ones.

*Going to this new eye doctor was the very best thing for me! I avoided a surgical procedure for glaucoma (which the other doctor probably would have performed). My new doctor said many people's eye pressure return to normal after the surgery, and I was one of them. No more drops!*

*The astigmatism was in both my cornea and natural lens, so the surgery reduced it in half. The astigmatism-correcting toric lens implant suggested by my first doctor could have caused me more problems because of that. There were a few other surgical procedures I avoided by going to this new doctor. I am totally convinced that God intervened in my mind and confirmed my decision to change doctors through my friends. I am so grateful!*

# Epilogue

## The One Event That Change My Whole Life

My story would have been completely different if my father's place of employment had not moved in the late 1960's. This one event was the catalyst for what I believe was God's plan for each member of my family.

Dad had a better job, with a much higher salary, and wonderful health insurance that was a true God-send with the massive medical bills for Mom, Emeline and himself. He became a more outgoing person in his job and church in Miami and later in Fort Myers. And he became a lot closer to the Lord and with Judy and me in his later years.

Mom had the most wonderful doctor in Miami, whom I believe God used to give her more time on this earth. The spiritual atmosphere in Miami enhanced her life and she influenced many people wherever she went. She lost that legalistic mindset she struggled with in New York.

Judy attended good schools and had Christian friends in her pre-teen and teenage years in Hialeah, and the influence of a good, spiritual church. She has quite a story through the years that is only hers to tell. Many Divine interventions.

As for me, the move from New York brought me into a 35-year career with the FAA, along with a salary I never dreamed I'd make and wonderful health insurance. This move changed this late bloomer into a person with growing confidence and a greater love for God and people. It greatly enhanced my social life and most importantly, eventually brought Dan and me together. As the journey continues, I believe God will continue His interventions as He guides my life.

Have I "arrived" in my Christian walk and in everyday situations? Certainly not! But the road I journey on is filled with a lot more grace and dependence on the Lord.

No one can ever convince me that God doesn't influence circumstances and use other people to accomplish His plan for my life. I've discovered that God is always at work behind the scenes of my life, but it really helps things when I cooperate with Him. To me, obedience is just cooperating with God, and is not so hard when I remember that He works everything together for my good!

You see, the bottom line is really a love relationship with God. It starts with acknowledging our inborn sinfulness which prevents intimacy with the Lord. All God requires is to repent and receive Jesus, God's Son who died for our sins, into our hearts. Then life can be led and blessed in this wonderful walk with God.

Do you know Him? If not, would you like to live an intimately God-guided and blessed life and absolutely know you are going to Heaven? The answers are on the next page.

# The ABC's of Knowing God Personally

# Through Jesus Christ

**A – Acknowledge** that you are a sinner and need God in your life, personally. The Bible says that *"All have all sinned and fall short of the glory of God."* (Romans 3:23). Living a "good" life, doing good deeds, or "not being a bad person" are not how we get to Heaven. Only God is holy, and sin (which we were born with) creates a separation that only Jesus can bridge for us. Everyone has a choice to make. Have you made yours?

*"The wages of sin is death, but the gift of God is eternal life in Christ Jesus our Lord."* (Romans 6:23)

**B – Believe** that Jesus died on the cross to forgive you and that He took the punishment for all of your sins upon Himself. This sacrificial atonement makes us clean before God and fit to have this wonderful, close relationship with Him. We do not earn God's free gift, and Jesus' resurrection from the dead brings us the hope of eternal life with Him in Heaven.

*"For God so loved the world that He gave His one and only Son, that whoever believes in Him shall not perish, but have eternal life."* (John 3:16)

Believing with your head is not the same as believing with your heart. God asks us to believe **in** His Son and connect with all He did and stands for.

**C – Confess** any sins that come to your mind, as well as your need of a life taken over by the holy God who loves you more than any human being can.

*"If we confess our sins, He is faithful and just and will forgive our sins and purify us from all unrighteousness."* (I John 1:9)

**Confess** your faith in Jesus Christ and ask Him to come into your heart. *"For it is with your heart you believe and are justified and it is with your mouth that you confess and are saved. For everyone who calls on the Lord will be saved."* (Romans 10:9-10, 13)

**D – Decide** to give Him your entire life. He is more than able to guide, protect and intervene in every area of your life.

*"Now to Him who is able to do immeasurably more than all we ask or imagine, according to His power that is at work within us."* (Ephesians 3:20)

**E – Eternal Life** begins the moment you accept Jesus into your heart.

*"But Christ has indeed been raised from the dead, the first fruits of those who have fallen asleep. For as in Adam all die, so in Christ, all will be made alive."* I Corinthians 15:20

John 10:10b quotes Jesus' words: *"I have come that they may have life and have it to the full."* Salvation is not just for gaining eternal life in heaven, but for the here and now.

～

A prayer to guide you:

Jesus, I know I need You in my life. I believe that you are the Son of God and died for my sins. Please forgive me of all of my sins and cleanse me of my sinful nature. Come into my heart to stay. I give my life over to You, believing that Your way is the only true way for my life. Thank you, in Jesus' name. Amen.

It's as simple as that! If you've prayed that prayer, please connect with a good church that preaches Christ and teaches the Bible. This is just the beginning of a Spirit-led life. We all need each other to grow in our faith.

And remember, this is not a life of perfection. This new life is lived with the Holy Spirit indwelling us. He guides us continually, but we need to stay close. We'll fall, but He'll pick us up every time. May God bless you as you have made this your prayer.

# Afterword

*"Then those who feared the Lord talked with each other, and the Lord listened and heard. A scroll of remembrance was written in his presence concerning those who feared the Lord and honored His name."* (Malachi 3:16)

How this book came to be is, I believe, another Divine Intervention. This came in stages, over a period of a few years. I'd written a letter to the daughter of my good friend, when she was desperately needing a job. I wanted to share with her how God led me to just the right job, but in stages. My friend was deeply touched that I would do this for someone I'd never even met. (She also told me that I write a very good letter.)

Then a year or so later when my niece was also needing a job badly, I remembered the letter I'd written to my friend's daughter, and sent Jenny a letter similar to that one. She, too, appreciated my letter.

Our 'lunch bunch' group of ladies from church often share how God has worked in our lives, and I thought how I'd like to share my entire story with them. But there's too much to tell and not nearly enough time. I certainly don't want to monopolize the conversation.

One morning I was thinking about this, and the words "why don't you write a book?" seemed to speak right into my consciousness. Was that God? I think so. I chewed on that thought awhile and then pushed it aside. Becoming an author hasn't been a burning desire, though I thought of writing about someone else, many years ago.

Perhaps what happened next was Divine intervention. While in the church library with nothing much going on at the moment, I googled Thomas Nelson, one of the publishers of the thousands of books we have. The first thing I saw was "Are you a first time author? Would you like to know how to go about writing and publishing a book?" I e-mailed my address to their division of WestBow Press – and the rest, as they say, is history!

∽

And the Divine interventions have continued –

In Community Bible Study, I was studying the return of Israel from exile, while also working on my story. We learned about Israel writing a "Book of Remembrance" (translated as "Book" in the New King James Version of the Bible). This was a result of their discovery of documents telling of God's acts of deliverance and faithfulness. Many of the people of Israel were brought back to God and then wrote a Book of Remembrance.

That brought my mind to create the sub-title for my story. I want my "Book of Remembrance" to encourage and bring people closer to the Lord.

∽

And so, the Divine interventions continue on....

# Acknowledgments

All through this process of writing my story, I have had Divine encounters with people who just 'happened' to be where I needed them to be. Some were total strangers, some I only casually knew. All encouraged, listened, gave suggestions and offered help. They were my 'angels'. I actually asked one outright if she was an angel!

Thank you, Cass Hahn, for encouraging me in the very initial stages of writing my story. Your prayers and support throughout mean so much!

Thank you Lige and Janice Jeter, for your listening ear and encouragement. Thank you Lige, for your constructive comments and suggestions to make my story much better from that raw, unpolished one at the beginning.

Thank you, Tamara Chilver, for your enthusiastic and helpful ideas in the later stages of my book. Watching and listening to you has been inspirational to me.

Thank you, Char Rafferty, for reading my story and giving me very encouraging reviews and comments. This meant so much, coming from an educator with a good eye for a story.

Thank you, Judy O'Halloran, for our spiritual and writers connection. God truly sent you to me in that 'chance' encounter while waiting in line at a book signing of a well-known author. You have been a great help and encouragement.

Thank you, Michelle Reader, for your prayer support and your great enthusiasm and listening ear throughout this past year. Your light-hearted, happy spirit has helped me not get too intense through this process.

Thanks many times over to Dan, my sweet husband, who has never complained about all the many hours I have spent in my office. Your encouraging review of the first and much later drafts of my story helped a lot!

But the greatest thanks goes to my Heavenly Father, who I believe has co-authored this book with me. There have been some things I haven't even remembered writing when I'd go through yet another review of the manuscript. May God receive the greatest glory from anything good resulting from this story of an ordinary life.